Power Health - Back to Basics

By

Dr. Martin P. Rutherford

ISBN: 1-4107-7547-X (e-book)
ISBN: 1-4107-7548-8 (Paperback)
ISBN: 1-4107-7546-1 (Dust Jacket)

Library of Congress Control Number: 2003094870

This book is printed on acid free paper.

Printed in the United States of America
Bloomington, IN

1stBooks - rev. 07/01/03

Acknowledgements

A book, and in this case, a multi-media educational program, does not just happen. This initial effort is the culmination of a lifetime of experiences, relationships and decisions. With each turn of events a new chapter was added. Though I am certain I will leave someone out, I would like to attempt to acknowledge everyone.

To my mother, thank you for giving me your determination, strength, courage and independence. Dad, I am sorry you won't see this but thanks for helping me to understand nothing comes over night and the old joke—"How do you get to Carnegie Hall?" Practice. Practice. Practice.

Mr. George Pentz, my Little League Baseball coach and still my friend for forty years. You were my first inspiration—it was you who taught me to set goals, organize, work hard and be fair.

Dr. Paul Fischer—it was you who made me realize I could be and do whatever I wished.

To Mrs. Freeman and Dr. Charlotte Lord: It was the two of you—my 6th grade teacher and college English teacher—who made me believe in myself and realize there was a brain in this head of mine.

To Chuck at 84 Lumber in Newport News, Virginia in 1975—Thanks for firing me! You got me off my lazy butt and forced me to pursue my dreams.

To Dr. Joseph Janse—president of my chiropractic college—a man of great dignity and class—it was you who made me realize that chiropractic was so much more than cracking backs. Many a day your kind words "helped me stay the course".

To Napoleon Hill, Stuart Wilde, Wayne Dyer, Dan Millman, Mark Victor Hanson, Ralph Waldo Emerson, Tony Robbins and Dennis Waitley - It was your works and lessons that have taught me, encouraged me, inspired me and helped me to slay my own dragons so that I might have the rich life experiences in this, and hopefully many other books, to share with my friends.

To my thousands of patients—Through your confidence and encouragement, inspiring me to become better at my craft, demanding that I fix you and answer your questions and allowing me to work at a profession that provides me acknowledgement and joy daily.

To Kevin Rick Anderson, my adopted stepson and co-producer of our Power Health Radio Show—We've had our battles but your respect, trust and confidence in me and your insights into my future in writing and speaking have been instrumental in creating and finishing this project.

To Quinn Anderson, my adopted stepdaughter—Your faith and pride in me are cause enough never to let you down.

To Joel Roberts, former Los Angeles Radio Personality and present day media coach for such luminaries as Chicken Soup for the Soul and Franklin Covey groups—it was you who first really made me believe I could do it all; then proceeded to show me how.

To Doug Stephan, national radio talk show host—The Doug Stephan Show - For showing me that fame and success is within our grasps and that class and down to earthiness can always be part of one's life.

To Trish Plank - You sustained me through the latter part of my quest by showing faith and encouragement that I could never have expected from one so experienced in the media field as you.

To Jana Wilde and Linda Shields—The two of you had more faith in me than I had in myself: that I could and would pull off a radio show and more. You both backed it up with faith. Thank you.

Thank you, Kevin Mirch, my friend and attorney. Though you still never return my phone calls, it was you who had the faith in me to introduce me to Robert Foreman and his wife, Linda. Linda, first, thank you for your kind words to Robert on my behalf, encouraging him to work with me. Thank you also for supporting my message.

To Robert Foreman—What can I say? You are one of the most talented people I know. Your original musical compositions and video production make my message take life and I am so grateful I have teamed up with such a neat guy. Without your input and encouragement this book would have been much longer in coming.

To Max McMannus, my personal trainer—You made our exercise video possible and you kept me in shape throughout the entire process. You are a 10—not an 8!

To Chris Blanton, cameraman for our Power Health Videos—You are a genius. Thanks for making me look ten years younger.

To my Office Staff—I have the world's best office staff. Their efficiency and dedication allowed me the time to focus on this project out of the office.

To ALL of my radio guests - You have allowed me to formulate the ideas in this educational program through "masterminding" with me on the air.

To Luke Stephenson—Just because you have always been a true friend.

To Dee Beaugez—I have not forgotten you. <u>None</u> of this would have occurred had you not "fatefully" teamed up again with Robert and saw the value of what we were trying to do. It was you who initially gave and continue to give life and direction to this and hopefully future projects.

As the saying goes, last but not least—Thank you to my wife, Nanja. For the last fifteen years, you have been the stability in my life. You have provided me with a serene, consistent home life while running our wellness office and allowing me to be all that I could be. Your faith and confidence in me is humbling and continues to inspire me to try harder to be who I am. Everyone I know thinks you are the brains behind our team and I think I'm beginning to agree. Thanks so much. I love you more than you will ever know.

Prologue

How do you stay healthy? Or better yet, how do you _get_ healthy? Is it diet? If so, which one do you follow? Or is it exercising? Should we be jumping up and down, "Spinning" ourselves silly, or let yoga contort us into pretzels? Maybe it's vitamins. Yeah, that's it—vitamins! Those will "fix us" right up. But what kind? How many? What dose? Confusing...

For twenty years people have come to me asking these questions and more. "What's the secret, Doc?" "How about that product?" "Can anyone really be healthy?" As a chiropractic physician, my practice has covered a wide spectrum from nutritional counseling to various modes of rehabilitation and even spiritual counseling. Always I consider it my responsibility to provide the answer. Frequently I had no answer. Humbling, and somewhat of a drag. Patients thought I should know the answers to these questions. The more I thought about it, I though so too. So ensued a multitude of never ending "research projects" to answer what seemed to be unanswerable questions.

One day a particularly desperate and chronically ill patient said, "What do _you_ do to stay so healthy?" Funny—I never thought of myself as all that healthy. "Yeah, well you're always so damned positive and you never get sick. You have tons of energy and you look ten years younger than your age." Really? Huh—give that patient a discount! "Maybe it is in your genes," she concluded.

Funny. I was <u>always</u> sick as a kid. Seemed like whatever came around I caught. And I always got it worse than anyone else. My mom was (and still is) a self-modeled home doctor. My dad was kind of a tough guy—no missing school just because you have got a 103° fever and vomited all night. We had the old fashioned doctor who came to the house, said some kind words and gave me a prescription to take. But my impression was always that I got better more or less on my bodies own capacity to heal and not particularly faster for all the intervention of my health care/medical "support" network.

And so it went. Vaccinations, tonsillectomy, stomach cramps, colds, flues, earaches, chicken pox, measles, mumps—you name it—I got it. I endured it. I recovered from it. Doctor's offices became my home away from home. I hated them. It was always the same. Show up early for my appointment. Wait an hour in the waiting room. Wait an hour in the treatment room. While waiting, I'm attired in one of those gowns that open in the back. Furthermore, I'm sitting on an ice cold exam table with tissue paper the only barrier between it and my bare butt. I'm hoping that every time I hear footsteps in the hall, it will be my door that opens next. It seemed like it never was. Finally, the grand entrance of God. The condescending attitude of the doctors who made believe (or maybe really thought) they knew my body better than me. Cursory exams and the prerequisite pronouncement of whatever they thought I had, followed by handing me a prescription that never worked. The scene played over and over again. Finally—I rebelled.

Rebellion did not sit well in my family. The conversation at family get-togethers frequently centered around whom was going to which doctor this week with what ailment and which new medicine was going to fix it. This was the 50's and the 60's. Medicine was going to wipe out disease with no effort needed on the part of the patient. It would be a brand new world. A pill, potion or lotion for your every health need. Criticism or questioning the medical profession and research community was akin to kicking Lassie. A new era was upon us and all would be well. The television said so.

I wasn't buying it. Though only 16, I just didn't <u>see</u> the big difference between the recovery from illness by people taking drugs and my recovering without them. People still seemed to get sick, take drugs, miss school, miss work, and eventually get better. It seemed to me that people were getting kind of wimpy. No one wanted to deal with any pain or body discomforts. We were in the era of drugs—all would and should be well. We had a <u>right</u> to be pain and illness free. What I was hearing and seeing didn't feel right. It was kind of spooky suddenly being in a society that seemed to be feeling it wasn't their responsibility to maintain their health and that if they didn't, there would be a pill to fix it. The drug companies said so—the newspapers said so, even the government said so. It must be true. And so it went.

My freshman year in college was spectacular. All American Honorable Mention in soccer. Seventh in the nation in batting averages in baseball and plenty of all that went with sudden athletic notoriety. But popularity had its price. Especially if you lack discipline which, at the time, I did. Parties and more parties. No sleep. Poor diet. Tons of stress. Next thing I know, I'm flat on my back. I was confined to bed with a severe case of mononucleosis and strep throat. I lost 35 pounds—I only weighed 152 pounds prior to the loss of weight—and almost died. Through it all I experienced a medical nightmare. Test, tests and more tests. All telling me how ill I was. Like I didn't already know? And drugs? Take this one - no, that one—no, this one is the new one. It should work! If it hadn't been such a nightmare, it would have been comical. But I was sick, really sick. I knew deep inside that I wasn't going to die. Much to everyone's chagrin, I stopped taking everything. I refused to see any doctors. Medications were history. I lay in bed, drank lots of water, prayed and focused on getting well. And to make a long recovery story short, I did. Get well, that is. The experiences and cognition that occurred during that recovery changed me forever and in the ensuing years were the basis of all that I pursued relative to sickness, disease and recovery. I discovered that <u>the power was within me</u>. And I have never wavered from that understanding in almost thirty years.

Yes, I am healthy—very healthy. But it did not come over night. Gaining optimum health was a process of trial and error, a journey through an alternative health care education culminating in a Doctorate of Chiropractic and over twenty years of practice and trying to help almost 20,000 people regain their own power to be free and healthy. Exploring the efficacy of herbs, drugs, vitamins, minerals, exercise, bodywork, Reiki, Jin Chin Jitsu—we have used it all at our healing arts center. At one point, I employed a naturopath, three chiropractors of differing techniques, a neurologist, a physical therapist and four massage therapists in a monumental experiment of trial and error to determine what worked best, what worked the worst, what were the true rules of getting and staying healthy, and how to simply communicate the findings to my patients and now to you the reader.

In the past few years, I have hosted scores of alternative health care professionals and experts on Power Health, an interactive, alternative health care radio talk show that seeks the unifying factors in sickness and healing. I've even spent six years sitting on the regulatory board of my profession and fourteen years involved in legislative activities on health matters to investigate the truth behind how health care decisions are made.

My conclusions—your best health insurance in the future will be not to get sick—and if you do get sick, to know how to heal yourself and utilize the body's healing system as simply as possible. Health and healing are simple and basic. The understanding of the principles necessary to be healthy and heal from sickness and disease are within the grasp of even the youngest child.

This book is my gift to you. These are the principles gleaned from thousands of hours of study, from experience of working with thousands and thousands of patients in a trial and error clinical setting, from personal experimentation, and from my desire to see every person feel and experience the health and personal freedom that I now enjoy.

This book, The Power Health Formula, and its accompanying tape series is the answer to my patient who asked, "What do you do to stay so healthy?" Use this formula and you can eliminate the confusion that you feel every day when you pick up the newspaper or watch television and hear about the newest study, about the next medicine, or about what you should or should not eat or do. Read this book, work this formula and I promise you that you will never need to read another health book again.

Contents

Personal Introduction

"Over all I'm pretty healthy, but you know, Doc, I'm tired. Tired all the time. No, I don't get much sleep. Insomnia, you know, kind of runs in the family. No, I don't drink very much and I eat a healthy diet. Oh yeah, I drink plenty of fluids. Exercise? I get plenty of exercise on my job. I'm on my feet all day. I hate my job, but it pays the bills. No, I don't really have the time to meditate or pray or be alone. I don't even have time for the spouse or the kids, really. When I am alone, it drives me nuts. My mind is going a million miles an hour and I just can't seem to stop it. It's part of the reason I can't sleep. Oh yeah, I've had several surgeries but I've recovered from them pretty well. Yeah, my back and neck hurt a little all the time. But so do my feet and knees. But after all, I'm not as young as I used to be, you know. I'm getting pretty old."

This is not a fictional patient. Worse yet, this is not an unusual patient. (We will call this patient "Patient U": the U stands for unhealthy and unaware.) The above patient is approximately 35 to 50 years old, doesn't have a fruit or vegetable on five out of seven days and on days when they do eat fruits and vegetables, it's usually only one serving. As a result of diet and lack of exercise, Patient U is generally about 25 to 35 pounds overweight and has started to develop structural problems in their lower neck, lower back and knees. These symptoms are due to muscular weakness and excessive forces of gravity (<u>fat</u>). Patient U smokes a half to one pack of cigarettes a day, has 14 to 25 glasses of alcohol in a week (but only drinks "occasionally") and drinks "lots of fluids". Rarely included in these fluids is water. Slightly more frequently, Patient U will have a glass of juice in the morning, one or two times a week. More frequently, Patient U drinks 6 to 20 cups of caffeine or decaffeinated coffee, diet or non-diet sodas with or without caffeine, or a similar quantity of the new designer ice teas on the market.

Patient U awakes from bed at the last possible minute after turning their alarm clock off two or three times. They race to feed the dog, put out the garbage, feed, wash, dress and take the kids to school. Then they race to work. Rarely has Patient U stopped for breakfast. In fact, rarely have they stopped. Most Patient U's arrive at work late or just on time for jobs that they hate or at the very least could do without. It is in this environment that they work, drinking coffee and eating donuts to "pick themselves up" because they didn't get any sleep last night. And so it goes, until the 5 o'clock whistle blows for some. Others work at their jobs long into the night or bring their work home. The evening hours and dinner in particular are a reward for the day. A reward of relaxation and vindication for a job well done—or at least done—under significantly stressful conditions.

Since Patient U hasn't eaten all day, he/she grabs a drink when they come in the door (which may be after soccer or baseball practice with the kids) then settles down to the only real meal of the day, a meal usually devoid of fruits and vegetables, but including alcohol, caffeine and sweets as the rewards of the day. Having eaten late, Patient U goes to bed with a full and uncomfortable stomach which along with the caffeine, alcohol and in many cases, nicotine, (we haven't even gotten to the prescription drugs yet) all combine to disturb the person's sleep patterns.

This is the patient who stands in front of me ten times a day, telling me: "You know, Doc, I'm really tired." Then asking me, "What could it be?" Generally Patient U is hoping for the silver bullet solution, like "Take St. John's Wort. That will do it." What's more, Patient U actually has truly convinced himself that, overall, he is healthy!!

I have learned, over the last twenty years, in dealing with Patient U not to:

1. Laugh at the patient.

2. Allow my jaw to drop and stare in disbelief, realizing they were not kidding.

3. Say something like, "You are pulling my leg, right?"

I've done all these things. With disastrous results, I might add. But I finally got it. Even with the enormous information (and disinformation) glut occurring over the last 25 years, Patient U still doesn't understand the very basic operating procedure of their body and has no concept of what true health entails.

In my mind, I reviewed my years of health educational classes in grades 1—12. I was unable to pull from my memory banks either of these concepts. Without these concepts, how can a person be healthy? My patients have no idea of what health really is, and even less of an idea about the basics of how the body operates. No wonder my patients weren't getting better. I remember the day this realization hit me. I was dumbfounded. Then I realized that Patient U didn't have the advantage of 5 years of schooling in a holistically oriented postgraduate school as well as years of clinical experience treating them. No one had ever really taught Patient U the basics. If anyone had tried, Patient U generally didn't have the time to learn as I soon found out.

Armed with my insights, observations and clinical trials as to why Patient U did or did not get well, I developed a basic operating manual for the human body, a formula if you will. I proceeded to teach this formula to my personal Patient U's and to Patient U's all over the country in more than 500 wellness classes. It has been an eye opening experience.

I discovered Patient U doesn't like to go to class for self-improvement any night of the week if he/she can avoid it. And does Patient U avoid it! I offered everything from health information packs to free

T-shirts to free X-rays to free treatments for Patient U to come to my class. These offers were made to every new patient who came to our offices. We had about a 30—35% attendance rate. Of those 30—35% that attended my wellness seminars, it was painfully obvious at the start of the class that 90% of these folks did not want to be there. The problem was becoming very apparent.

However, a very interesting phenomenon occurred during the course of our 1½ hour wellness class. As people began to realize there was no hook or backend products for them to buy, the information I was providing began to sink in. My Patient U's started doing an interesting thing. They not only started to listen and become interested, they started to get excited. During post class question and answer periods, it became obvious that Patient U had never understood what constitutes the very basics of health, how their bodies operated, how do you get sick and how do you get well and what they were doing to "sugar up the gas tank" and cause their bodies to not operate properly. Patient U became most excited at gaining the understanding that as long as there's so much as a spark of life in a dysfunctional or "sick" body, that the sickness process can usually be reversed using a simple formula that is easy to understand and very easy to do for people of all ages. What most affected my Patient U's was that they left the class feeling not only excited but more importantly <u>empowered</u>. Empowered by the knowledge that they controlled their bodies and at this point, it may sound silly, but also their destiny. Think about it—if you can't control what happens in your body, how can you control anything else in your life? Knowledge in this case is control and control is <u>power</u>. Personal power that you can only know when you feel and experience it. And so the Power Health Formula developed. By the way, those 30—35% of the patients who came to the Power Health classes got better more frequently and had quicker results than those who didn't attend the class. To date, thousands have attended, providing me with invaluable clinical trial information and conclusions that I'm dedicated to sharing with you. In the following pages, you will learn all you need to know about being healthy. I'm told it's all been said before. If that is true, then somebody has not gotten it because I'm still treating tons of sick people. Most recent statistics indicate that as much as 80—90% of all sicknesses and diseases—including heart attacks, strokes and cancer—are <u>life</u> <u>style</u> diseases and are <u>totally</u> preventable.

To that end, I'm going to make one more stab at bringing this information to a wanting and needy public in a format that has been helping my patients for the last 20 years. The Power Health Formula is my gift to you. It is real. It works. If you use it as your bible, it is likely to be <u>all</u> the health information you will ever need.

Enjoy.

Health—What is it?

In hundreds of public talks and presentations, "What is Health" has been my hook. In radio and speaking the hook wakes you up. It engages your interest and gets you thinking about what is health? So, let's think about what health is. And isn't.

What Health isn't

Is it feeling good? If so, what is that? Is it having lots of energy? Not really, you can get that from drugs. Is it the absence of symptoms and/or pain? I don't think so. It can take seven to ten years for a cancer tumor to cause symptoms. Was that person really healthy during those seven years of no pain or symptoms? I don't think so.

Maybe health is just not being sick that day. I have patients who smoke, drink excessively, don't exercise, can't sleep, have had several organs removed, look me straight in the eye and say, "...but otherwise, Doc, I'm really healthy." Or maybe health is a tri-athlete pounding out 80 to 120 miles per week while spending six hours in the gym and umpteen hours swimming and biking? Nope. Too extreme, trust me. In the long run, the professional athlete pays a steep price.

And, speaking of health, can we get it in a bottle of Androstiendione, Ibuprofen, Metabolife, Prozac, Valium or from a daily aspirin? Nope!

1

What about herbs, vitamins and minerals? The answer to all of the above is NO. Health does not come in a bottle. EVER!

So if it is not in a bottle, where is it? I will tell you where it is. It is hiding. Where? In YOU!! That's right, the health you do so desperately crave, is already in that body of yours. All <u>YOU</u> have to do is let it out!

What health is

Health is having all of the cells in our body working at maximum efficiency and in optimum balance, thus giving us the maximum operating and healing potential at all times.

That's a mouthful. But get it. Because this is what true health is. And <u>you</u> can accomplish true health by following the basic, simple and complete Power Health Formula. The Power Health Formula is a law; it is all you will ever need. If you don't believe me, check it out for yourself.

> *"I find it odd that a lot of people who get involved with spiritual work and healing want to throw away their bodies to reject or escape the physical plane. They think everything to do with the physical plane is bad. Yet we have chosen to be born to a physical level for a reason. We have to live consciously in a physical body. That does <u>not</u> mean throwing away our bodies. It means understanding our bodies and treating them with great reverence."*
> *Lynne Andrews—Author*
> *A Native American Medicine Woman*

Understanding Our Organisms (Better Known as Bodies)

Our bodies are self-regulating, balancing organisms that are self-contained and have evolved as a part of, <u>not separate from,</u> nature. The cell is our body's basic unit and our health is a reflection of the state of functioning of our cells and their response to the environment. Here's how it all works.

In the beginning, a body is formed by two cells—the sperm and the egg—getting together to form one cell. That cell immediately begins to divide into 2, then 4, then 8 cells, etc. until it becomes a complete body of 50 to 70 trillion cells. Neat trick, huh? It gets better. These cells, through a variety of processes, develop into several more specialized cells and ultimately into systems: cardiovascular, digestive, hormonal, nervous, genitourinary, respiratory, immune, and more. These systems have evolved over a period of <u>millions</u>, if not <u>billions</u> of years.

Your organism's, or body's, if you prefer, intricate and interacting complex systems developed from <u>eons</u> of evolutionary trial and error to create an incredibly <u>perfect</u> machine. To understand your body, how it gets sick and how it gets well, it is vital to acknowledge the inner wisdom of the body. Billions of years, changes, deaths and lives have created the unfathomable, perfect self-adjusting balancing process called homeostasis, and your innate healing ability.

> *"These healing forces automatically activate within a fraction of a second, some more slowly. If a man hemorrhages, his body pulls water from his system into the circulatory system; this keeps blood pressure from dropping below critical levels. When a woman is suffering frostbite, her body has automatically adjusted by slowing the blood flow to her fingers and toes, ears and nose, reserving heat and oxygen for the all important brain and organs in her chest and abdomen. This internal equilibrium can adapt itself to a temperature change of even a fraction of a degree, bathing the body in cooling perspiration when it becomes warm and when cold, prompting shivers to convert energy to heat."*
> <u>The Incredible Machine</u>, 1986.
> *Pages 10—11*

The regulating balancing mechanisms extend to tens of thousands of physiological and structural processes. Of these, it's most important for you to understand your body's immune response.

"We live in a world dense with microbes: bacteria and viruses, parasites and fungi abound in the air, water, and soil and on the living things around us. Most of these organisms have little interest in the human species. But a specialized few find the human body an inviting habitat: warm, protected, and well stocked with nutrients. Some settle into the nose and ears, some on the skin and in the intestinal tract.

"Usually we live in harmony with these microscopic residents, most stay on the body's surfaces. But under certain conditions—when we are <u>malnourished</u>, <u>exhausted</u>, <u>injured</u>, or under <u>severe</u> <u>stress</u>, resident organisms and other microbes may invade and multiply in our tissues, or set forth in the blood stream, traveling to all parts of the body. If unchallenged, they can cause serious, even fatal, afflictions.

"Considering the number of potential interlopers, <u>disease</u> <u>occurs</u> <u>very</u> <u>rarely</u>. This is no accident. Nearly every human possesses a sophisticated and efficient system that works 24 hours a day in every part of the body (and in every cell—my addition) to ensure good health. Known as the immune system, this network of cells and organs responds almost instantaneously to the presence of any disease, chasing intruders, mustering its forces to halt the progress of a polio virus or to thwart the effects of a meningococcus bacterium. We rely on this powerful system not just to repel disease-causing microbes, but to keep house inside the body. Good health depends on order and consistency among the body cells, tissue, and organs. The immune system preserves this state of balance by removing dead or damaged cells and by seeking out and eliminating wayward or mutant cells."

The Incredible Machine, 1986.
Page 157

So what's the point? The point is—now get this: <u>You are enough</u>! All tools and mechanisms that you need to experience powerful health are already in place and working within your body. Those that are not, are available through your "innate wisdom" or "spirit", which we will discuss later.

What is the secret to naturally abundant health, energy, balance and peace of mind? Like Frances Bacon said, "We need to obey nature." We need to get in tune with and follow the laws that will allow our body to perform optimally. Numerous think tanks and scientific organizations throughout the world have acknowledged that 85% (and I believe it's closer to 99%) of the world's sickness and disease are "life-style related". The big three: cancer, stroke and cardiovascular disease are no doubt 100% caused by lifestyle inadequacies. So why aren't we handling this situation? Because we are confused, uncertain and overwhelmed by the glut of mass information that attacks us daily via the media, television, radio, newspapers, "health magazines", books and the Internet. All provide solutions. But those solutions usually conflict and contradict each other. Most have a hidden agenda that is not in your best interest. To whom do you turn? Where do you start?

In treating some 20,000 patients at our office, we have found that most patients are paralyzed from taking action to achieve optimum health. Meat or no meat? Salt or no salt? Vitamins or no vitamins? Exercise: what type, what kind? Is there an answer in science and its drugs? Confused and paralyzed by fear and doubt, not wanting to waste time and/or money, the typical patient does nothing until their organism (body) reaches a point where it can no longer compensate, loses its balance and gets "sick". That's when they come to me, the doctor.

It doesn't have to be that way and if you follow the Power Health program, it won't be that way for you. The Power Health Formula is all you will ever need. Because the program does what no other program does for you. It lays down the law. Simple, clear and concise. Black and white. What law? The natural, physical and spiritual law of how to keep that magnificent body of yours (yes, there's a magnificent body in there, believe it or not) working optimally so it can do what it's already naturally designed to do in this universe: namely keep you healthy, energetic, stress free and happy.

"But doc, I'm really sick. How's your formula going to help me?" Well, it's the same formula for getting well as for obtaining optimum health. A law is a law. It works on planet Earth and on Mars (take gravity, for instance) and it works all the time. Your body follows the same laws in sickness and in health.

Your body is continually replacing its atoms and cells. Your body is not static. It is in a continually changing dynamic state. Some stomach cells replace themselves every few minutes, while the heart muscle, skin and liver cells replace themselves from every few weeks to every few months. I have read estimates that every atom in your body is replaced every 2 to 7 years depending on the reference source. What does that mean? It means with the body constantly changing and you following the Power Health Formula/Law for optimum cellular function, you will be replacing sick and damaged cells and atoms with new, normally balanced and optimally functioning cells that will allow your immune system and other balancing mechanisms to do their job of getting your body well, and keeping it well.

Remember your body's natural response is to heal. Just cut your finger and observe the natural healing response. You follow the Power Health Formula to get well. You follow the same Power Health Formula to stay well. It's all in the Formula. There is nothing missing.

So now that we understand health, what it is, how the body works, how it gets sick and how it gets well, let's get to the Power Health Formula and get on with it.

F.I.R.M. The Power Health Formula

You are part of a process that has been evolving since the beginning of time. The universe was created and has expanded and evolved according to exact specific principles. The human body has also been created and evolved within those very same principals. Though the process of creation and evolution maybe complex and controversial the principals that guide the evolution and proper functioning of the human body are not. Within your magnificent body is an entire universe of its own with hundreds of millions of organisms perfectly coexisting in a biochemical balance that—when maintained, allows you optimum health and the optimum mechanisms to adapt to and overcome sickness and disease. Millions of chemical reactions and hundreds of thousands of chemical pathways are operating 24 hours, 7 days a week 365 days a year for your entire life in a delicate dance to keep your organisms in your body in top working order. You don't have to know or understand anything about the intricacies or complexities of these systems to gain the benefits of their existence and efficiency. All you have to do is follow the law that the universe demands of you to keep it all in order and balance and not interfere with its process of keeping you well. The Power Health Formula is the law. It's been gleaned from the key laws that govern the discoveries of Einstein's relativity and Stephen Hawking's black holes. Yet it is not complex—it's simple.

You probably fall into one of two categories. 1) you are not healthy and are so overwhelmed by health information that you are paralyzed and don't know what to do or where to start on your journey to health, power and control or 2) You are relatively healthy and are being aware of the fact that there is more. This person is taking 85 supplements per day and owns every exercise machine known to man and still feels there is something missing. Oh yes—candidate number two is even more stressed out than candidate number one due to trying to stay on a program that cannot be maintained for long.

The Power Health Formula handles it all. The formula is: Fuels + Interconnected Highways + Rest + Mental Power Control = Health

Simple huh? Then why isn't everyone doing it? The components of the formula are what the universe, nature, and life demands of you in return for getting your machine to work optimally. And that is what you are. An intelligent machine. A machine that needs the proper high-octane fuels for maximum performance, that needs the proper structure and function to allow it to work efficiently. A machine that needs rest (I don't believe they've invented a perpetual motion machine that never wears out have they) and a machine that needs the proper mind set to program and run it efficiently and effectively.

Follow this formula and you will get antioxidants, anti-aging, detoxification, 95% less risk of stroke, cardiovascular disease, and cancer. You can decrease your dependence on doctors, drugs, surgeries, and even herbs, vitamins, and minerals. You'll lose weight, be less stressed, sleep better, and be in more control. You'll be what the universe law predicts you will be if you follow the law: healthy, self sufficient, happy, successful, and powerful. Follow the law and being "healthy" is inevitable.

Don't believe it? Turn the page, start applying the principals. In three months you will understand the power of going with the flow of the universal law of health and you will feel better than you have in years.

F Stands for Fuels

The human body is like a high powered, high performance Daytona 500 race car. My guess is that you are reading this book because your body is performing more like a '56 Chevy pickup truck (no offense to Chevy fans). We are about to change that. In addition to being well engineered, high performance racecars, like your body, demand high performance, clean, efficient fuels. Certainly you would not dream of putting cheap gas into Mario Andretti's racecar. And it would certainly be considered sabotage to put sugar in his gas tank. Mario would probably have you put in jail.

I wish it were that way with the human species and our bodies. But it's not. Most us put cheap fuel, including tons of sugar, in our bodies 21 or more times a week—morning, noon and night.

Food is your organism's fuel. Without fuel, your car stops running. Without food your body would not run very long. Poor food/fuel products prevent the human machine from running optimally. Poor food/fuel products contribute to illness and physical breakdown. Practitioners of the Chinese, East Indian and American Indian schools of healing scrutinize patient diet - or the lack thereof - first. They do this for a good reason. More than 85% of illnesses, including the big three, are caused by lifestyle. A major part of that lifestyle is food.

So, the Power Health Formula starts with F, which stands for fuel (food). The first law is—good fuel is necessary for good health.

9

Food? Seems rather obvious. But in a country where food is almost too abundant, over half the population is overweight, and fast food reigns supreme, fuel could well be the most important element of the formula. Want to raise your energy level quickly? Clean up your diet! Lose weight? Eat the right foods. Please notice that I didn't say to eat less food. The proper foods/fuels will positively reduce your stress level and do much more.

Let's look at all that I am sure you want from a health program and how you can get it inexpensively from proper fuels. You can achieve these results without drugs, vitamins, herbs, minerals or weight loss programs.

Detoxification

The detoxification craze has been sweeping the alternative field for years. Colonics, fasting, cleanses sweat lodges and more. You know what? They all work. But always remember that you are enough— you are whole. You can avoid all of these and still achieve maximum health by simply putting the optimum fuel into your body.

Among those innumerable balancing mechanisms in your body, the process of detoxification occurs through the blood, kidneys, bowels, skin and more. These are your built in mechanisms. Part of what your body needs to help that system work optimally is to provide it with plenty of fiber. And where does that fiber come from? Not from psyllium seed. At least not ideally. It comes mostly from fruits and vegetables. Both are composed largely of cellulose fibers. These cellulose fibers not only regulate the rate at which nutrients enter your system, but also create bulk in your bowels allowing them to be swept clean and act as part of your detoxification system.

What's best? A 70% vegetable, fruit and grain diet. Look at your plate. 70% of what is on your plate should be vegetables, fruits and grains. That's it. Simple. We could probably stop right here with our diet recommendations. This single dietary recommendation would improve your health significantly. But there is more.

Stress Reduction

If your body is working optimally, your mental stresses are much easier to deal with. In fact, much of what you perceive as stress is physical. This is particularly true on those days when you are stressed out but "do not know why". That subtle feeling of underlying fear or uncertainty that you can't connect to anything "mental". Diet related stress is a function of the quantity and quality of food and the elimination or balancing of specific ingestible substances.

Quantity of Food

Eating too much food at one sitting causes physical stress. Your body is a highly adaptable organism that is designed to handle small quantities of food. If you stuff it with more than it can handle, two things happen: you get fat and you overtax all of its organ system. Both cause your system to become unbalanced, making it work harder to digest, assimilate and eliminate the excess food. While this is physical stress, it registers in your brain on a subconscious level simply as stress.

Quality of Food

There are certain substances that are natural physiological stressors. These include: sugar, salt, caffeine, alcohol, nicotine and many prescription drugs. Eliminate or drastically reduce these in your diet. This is vital to understand. Too much sugar alters your blood sugar which affects the nerves and can cause nervousness, headaches, tiredness and depression. Too much salt can cause water retention and high blood pressure. Caffeine, alcohol and nicotine all affect your nervous system directly, causing nervousness, anxiety, the jitters, ringing in the ears, sleep deprivation and more. Yes studies show that a combination of caffeine and alcohol may reduce the risk of heart disease. But is it worth the tradeoff of creating physiological stress and the risk of their effects on other systems?

Not only does all of this make you physically stressed but it causes you to be less able to handle your non-physiological, emotional, stresses (like your job, husband, wife, mom, kids, boss, etc.).

11

A good rule of thumb for any substance is if it goes into your body and causes an imbalance (increased heart rate, depression of mental clarity, nervousness, "acid indigestion", etc.), it either does not belong in your system or it is required in reduced quantities and for medicinal purposes only. The same goes for certain foods. If hot, spicy foods cause heartburn and indigestion or do not eliminate well, then do not eat them! Duh! Remember that your body is unique. It's up to *you* to pay attention and listen to *your* body. Not your ego that says—I want that even if it kills me! Simple huh?

So how do you eliminate these physical stresses? First, eat several small meals each day. Stop immediately when your hunger has been satisfied. Pay particular attention to what you are eating when dining out or while chatting with a spouse or friend. Second, eliminate totally or severely restrict all caffeine, alcohol, nicotine, drugs, unnatural sugars, salt and any food that causes imbalance and stress. What you don't put in your body is equally as important as what you do!

Anti-Aging

Now here's a new buzzword. First of all, you do not anti-age. We do however get out of shape and use incorrect fuels to corrode our organisms. We are all going to age and we are all going to die. Most studies indicate that 115 years is a realistic life goal and that is probably as old as one could get. We age faster than that because we are constantly losing our battle with the environment. Why? Because we continuously violate nature's laws and do not follow the Power Health Formula. Follow the formula and your body will "anti-age" or, in my view, age better.

What fuels contribute to keep the cells functioning optimally and anti-age? Fruits and veggies. Heard that one before? Boring, huh? Well, you can eat fruits and veggies (which are loaded with the now famous antioxidant substances that stop your cells from "rusting" and are considered highly preventive for cancer) or you could take antioxidant supplements. I choose the food. Again, 70% of your daily intake of fuels should include fruits and vegetables.

Weight Loss

This is the number one issue in America today. We know that weight loss helps energy levels, back, knee and digestive problems, self-image, depression and the big three—cancer, heart disease and strokes. There are drugs, natural stimulants, fat farms and weight loss centers. It is a billion dollar industry—<u>your</u> dollars! It is crazy and it does not work. There are two and <u>only</u> two components to losing weight. Eating right (I did not say less) and exercise. Every semi-sane diet that "works" has these elements in common:

- eating several small meals per day—controls appetite.

- calorie restriction—with several small meals of the correct fuels you can reduce calories and eliminate hunger, while probably having a difficult time consuming the sheer volume of foods.

- lots of fruits, vegetables and grains- coincidentally about 70% of your diet - even on high protein diets.

- keep protein portions to 15 to less than 30 grams/meal based on sex, weight and activity level (steak, chicken, fish—the size of a deck of cards)—that is all your system can assimilate at each feeding anyway (a piece of protein about the size of your hand.)

- drink lots of H_2O.

The rest of the elements of <u>all</u> these famous diets is theory, BS and marketing hype. The above are basics. Forget about high carb, low carb, high protein, low fat. It is about <u>balance</u>, everyone. It has been about <u>balance</u> for 40 million years. It is not going to change any time soon.

It is so simple, it is stupid. And that is what I need. Simple. These eating rules/laws will increase your energy, help you to lose weight, regulate stress, prevent lifestyle diseases and most of all, will allow that high powered, high performance machine of yours to purr, balancing all systems and taking the first step to Power Health.

Energy

Who isn't tired today? It is the number one complaint among my patients and a symptom of every disease known to man. The best and quickest way to raise your energy—bar none—is proper eating habits. Proper eating habits:

- Eliminate overwork for the digestive and cardio-vascular system. This conserving energy delivers appropriate nutrients to the cells and organs providing them high octane fuels. This keeps the engine running smoothly, stops it from clogging and regulates blood sugar. Blood sugar regulates the nervous system. The nervous system regulates just about everything in the body. The result is a boost in energy levels.

- Eliminate the drains on your systems. The number one dietary energy booster is to eliminate or relegate to no more than one "party day" per week, alcohol, caffeine and nicotine (including cigars). Do this and watch your energy skyrocket. If you are worried about being a bore, rest assured most people will respect and admire you. Many will ask you "Where did you get so much energy?" Suck it up, go through withdrawals, stop the excuses, do not go to a twelve-step program. JUST DO IT! You will be a born again human. I guarantee it.

Notice we did not include drugs, ginseng, vitamin B or natural uppers. In fact, your increased energy depends more on what you don't put in the engine than what you do.

SOME FREQUENTLY ASKED QUESTIONS ABOUT DIET

What about red meat?

It is not a big deal if you eat red meat once or twice a week. I can hear the screams from the veggie only group already but, as long as meat is lean, even patients with high cholesterol levels should feel free to choose either red or white meat as part of a healthy diet.

Dr. Michael H. Davidson, of the Chicago Center for Clinical Research in the Archives of Internal Medicine, reported the results of his team's study. The investigators examined changes in blood cholesterol in nearly 200 men and women counseled to follow the federal government's National Cholesterol Education Program Heart Healthy Diet for 36 weeks. This is considered a low fat diet. Subjects were directed to consume either six ounces of lean beef, veal, or pork, or six ounces of chicken or fish per day for five to seven days a week.

By the end of the study, total cholesterol levels had decreased by 1.0% in patients assigned to lean red meat and by 1.8% in those assigned to lean white meat. Reduction in LDL's ("bad") cholesterol were 1.7% in patients eating primarily red meat and 2.9% in those eating primarily lean white meat. Concentration of HDL ("good") cholesterol—thought to help protect against heart disease—increased 2% in both groups. No significant change in triglyceride levels was observed in either group.

The key here is balance and moderation. If you are eating it a few times a week with lots of steamed veggies and salads—in the above quantities—enjoy it! Savor it. Our digestive systems have spent at least 6 million years of trial and error figuring out how to break red meat down and use it. If you are one of the small percentage of people who cannot digest red meat, you will find out quickly. Eat red meat with a 50% to 70% veggie and fruit diet. If red meat is not for you, you will know within four days. You will be lethargic, sluggish and have difficulty with elimination. If that is you, stick to chicken and fish. You NEED protein. If you choose a vegetarian route, you MUST eat tons of soy, tofu, etc. to get enough protein. If you eat meats—red, poultry or fish—opt for organic free range. Most markets now carry them. And the extra cost is worth the cleaner product. Oh yes, relative to utilizing the entire Power Health Formula if you eat red meat in moderate quantities you can (cast) away your fears relative to insecticides, pesticides, hormones, antibodies etc. your body can handle it.

What about people who are vegetarian for spiritual or philosophical reasons?

The two oldest health traditions in the world are the Chinese and Avervedic (Indian) Health Disciplines. Both traditions acknowledge that only a small percentage of people, certainly no more than 25%, are physiologically equipped to live on a strictly vegetarian diet. I do not believe it is that high. This fact, not a theory, has evolved from six to seven thousand years of trial and error. It is the most reliable information available on the subject. Your body is your body. It must obey the natural law and your evolution. It is not aware of your religious or spiritual beliefs or whether you believe in evolution or not. See the previous section on red meat to determine what category of food your body requires. Then you must decide.

What about all the information that that says I cannot get the appropriate vitamins and minerals from foods and that I must use supplements?

The problem with all of the information, which you are exposed to every day, is it is disseminated totally out of context. Mostly by business entities whose agenda is to get you to use their supplemental products. In addition it can practically be argued that all studies conducted on human beings are incomplete because you can never account for all of the factors that influence the human physiology. The information you get states: people are deficient in vitamins and minerals. Most of you take them to protect yourselves from some disease or the aging process. What the information from the studies does not tell you is that the person who was low in vitamins only eats one vegetable per week, smokes (killing the vitamins), drinks alcohol (killing the vitamins), drinks caffeine (killing the vitamins), doesn't exercise, doesn't sleep well, and is stressed out of his/her mind (killing the vitamins). You can get sufficient nutrients from your food if you eat the proper fuels in the sufficient quantities. In fact it's the only way to get all nature has to offer. Aside from fact that science can't agree on correct daily amounts of individual supplements and vitamins it is agreed that science doesn't even know of all of the existing nutrients currently available from our food.

Food is only one part of the Power Health Formula. If you perform all the parts of the Formula, you will see that they work in synch to maximize the use of your food and preserve the vitamins and minerals you are using. This is contrary to the view of one prominent M. D. turned alternative health care guru who just recently stated in one of his newsletters, "Many intelligent people in our society still believe the nonsense that you can get all the nutrients you need from optimum diet alone." Well, I am one of those intelligent people. I also feel it is a salient point here that this particular health care guru promotes his own line of vitamins.

I discuss who does and does not need vitamins according to what part of the health gradient you belong to later in the book. I'm high on the health gradient. I do not use vitamins or minerals except when I am under extended periods of physical demand. I do follow the Formula. I am the healthiest, most energetic person I know. If you are working your way up the Formula take a multivitamin/mineral and see how you feel. If you feel better, keep taking them until the program kicks in. If you do not feel a difference, finish the bottle or chuck them out, but do not buy more. Also do not take a variety of vitamins on your own. Your system is complex and delicately balanced. An increase in one substance in the body creates numerous balancing reactions to take place. Follow the Power Health Formula and relax!

What is Proper Eating?

My intention here, as always, is to break eating down into its simplest elements. I have read every diet plan known to man. Aside from the fact that most of the now famous diet books have produced vast followings and some results, their success, in my opinion has been largely due to giving horribly fed people some reasonable guidelines to follow and then marketing the crap out of the product. If a million people use the - whatever the new fad diet is—book and follow it, some will get results. These results become miracle testimonials and miracle testimonials are marketing diamonds. Usually the diet book promotes the last new or rehashed diet theory to catch our interest and then promotes a basically sound diet with some variation and debate on the frequency of feeding and the amounts of proteins,

17

carbohydrates and fats that should be consumed. Thus they all get some percentage of results.

In twenty years, I have watched these diets come and go. I have observed that whenever a new diet hits the market about 25% to 35% of the devotees' get "miracle" results. They are usually the patients who are so far gone dietarily that any positive change would have made an improvement. The book release just happened to coincide with a point in their life when their priorities had changed and they had the motivation to do something about their diet. The miracle results usually come from this new found discipline and focus as well as having a somewhat rational plan to follow. It is also a known fact that any drug or any drug therapy has about a 30% placebo affect. Interesting, huh? I do not find offense with most of the new fad diets whether they are McDougal, Atkins, Zone, Blood type, or Protein. Despite all the debate on protein rich versus carbohydrate rich versus fat rich, they are all much better than the standard American diet and will **all** get some percentage of varying results from nominal to spectacular—if you follow their diet plan.

There lies my problem. Complexity. I cannot help it. If it is complex, my brain turns off. Figuring out Blood types, protein amounts, carbohydrate amounts, philosophy of vegetarian versus red meat versus chicken—it is all too complex for me. Thus I either will not do the diet or I will not do it for very long. These diets all contain two elements we do not need in our already overly, technologically stressed lives—complexity and lack of balance. They are all extreme and the universe abhors extremes.

We are about to change this situation to give you the simplest diet plan ever. It will contain all of the effective elements and if you happen to be ready for it and are in the mind set to follow it—you will get the same results with less effort, confusion and expense. Here we go.

The (not so secret) Secrets of the Human Diet

Eat several (5-6) small meals per day. We are not going to talk calories because you are only going to eat slowly and STOP EATING when your body is no longer hungry.

If at one of your feedings you are not hungry, **don't eat**. Simple—I know—but people tend to eat "when it is time" instead of when they are hungry. Remember caloric restriction is supposedly the only scientifically, proven dietary recommendation that prolongs life. We eat too many calories mainly because we pay attention to taste and ignore the fact that we eat beyond satisfaction of our appetite or we eat in response to some emotion. If you eat 5—6 times per day only until you are no longer hungry, you will lose weight, extend life and not be hungry. If you want to buy a calorie counter and eat according to the calorie chart located at the end of the chapter—fine (This is for you engineering, computer, accountant types). But if you just stop eating when your full its really not necessary.

Do whatever you can to have 70% of your diet be fruits and veggies and grains—for the rest eat exactly what you want your protein will work itself out. It will work out. Honest. Taken in context of the entire Power Health Formula, you will be fine. You will eat meats/fish/chicken and some desserts. Whatever you like. Eyeball your meal. If 70% of the total volume on your plate contains fruits and veggies and grains, you will be fine.

Drink tons of water—8 to 12 glasses per day.

Oh, yeah. Enjoy every bite of food you put in your mouth. In other words, slow down. Chew your food, get those "natural" digestive enzymes working for you, and taste it! Put your fork down between each mouthful. Relax and enjoy.

Stay out of fast food joints.

Only shop the perimeter of the supermarket. This is where the real food is located. Only venture into the aisles for dry goods.

19

That is it. That is enough. People who eat like this are usually healthy, energetic, happy and—oh, yeah—<u>thin</u>. Do just what I say. Do not try to complicate it. Remember—simple is powerful!

Additional Healthful and Simple Diet Recommendations

Increase fruits and vegetables minimum of 50%, preferably 70% of your diet. This increases antioxidants, fights cancer, reduces need for vitamins and it is cheap. Remember 5 to 11 helpings per day. (1 fruit = 1 helping, 1 cup of veggies = 1 helping, 1 salad = 1 helping, French fries are not included in this formula)

Remember to include fats in your diet. If you are a non-vegetarian, you will find that you will get most of your fats from the meats that you eat. If you wish to add fat to your diet, keep it minimal. A small amount of fat goes a long way. A teaspoon full of olive oil on a salad is more than enough to fulfill your fat requirement for any dinner or lunch.

Stick to chicken, fish and turkey as much as possible and keep the red meats to a minimum (2x's a week) although you need not eliminate them entirely. If you are a vegetarian make sure you are eating enough protein products such as soy, tofu and nuts.

Try not to eat any heavy meals especially at lunch. Heavy meals make your digestive system work overtime and tire you out. Make your dinner light, so that digestion ultimately does not interfere with sleep and increase weight gain. You will get the feel for what meals give you that heavy feeling and which don't in approximately 1-3 weeks of beginning the Power Health Program.

If it causes indigestion, gas or heartburn **do not eat it**. <u>Duh</u>!

Smoking, caffeine and alcohol alter your physiology. Eliminate or reduce their use dramatically. You already <u>know</u> this to be true so do not be swayed by debate on the benefits of these drugs.

Characteristics of a Natural Human Eater

Food is food—it is a fuel and nothing else. People who eat well eat to live. Most of us live to eat. Eat to eat. Most overweight people use food as a reward or emotional medication. I'm happy—let's eat; I'm sad—let's eat. Like I said above, if you are hungry then eat. If you are not, do not eat. If you need a guideline, do 5 to 6 small meals per day. Eating should not be a major event in your life in your life, just fuel for the machine.

Natural eaters usually eat what they want to eat and usually in small quantities. When they are hungry, they eat what they want, eat until they are satisfied and leave the rest on their plate. You will never see one of these people drive down the street and suddenly turn into a donut shop because the sign made them want food. They do not view food as anything other than "fuel".

Natural eaters are conscious of what they are eating and conscious of how hungry they are. They are paying attention. A Natural Human Eater will never look down at their plate and wonder who ate their dinner or not be able to remember what they just ate! These people decide what to eat and enjoy every bite. Their intestines are satisfied more quickly because in enjoying their food and concentrating on it they chew their food longer and the stomach and the intestines get satisfied sooner.

Pick up a raisin. Take a minute. Look at it. I mean really look at it. See its color, curves etc. Now feel it and smell it. No, really, I mean it. Feel its texture and smell its fragrance. Now put it in your mouth and chew it—let us say 32 times just for the heck of it. Tastes good, huh? (That's those digestive enzymes you never gave a chance to do their jobs). Probably the best tasting raisin you have ever had! Why? Because you were there. You paid attention to it. You savored it.

Natural Human Eaters are satisfied with less because they enjoy their food more. Eating consciously is like any other discipline or sport. The mechanics are difficult to master at first but once you learn, it becomes "second nature". Pay attention to your food slow down and enjoy it.

21

Natural Human Eaters use the words "I am full." I hate it when I tell someone I have finished eating and they continue to pressure me to eat with—"Oh, come on, just a little more?" Learn to say, "I am full". Natural Human Eaters leave food on their plates, even in expensive restaurants. Food is important to these humans as a fuel not as a sensual experience or an emotional attachment. Natural Human Eaters treat food as their servants not as their masters.

Be an 8—not a 10. What do I mean by this? Let us say on a scale of 1 to 10, 1 is poor dietary habits and 10 is perfection. Do not be perfection. It is not necessary. If you follow the diet of recommendations in this book 80% of the time, you will be fine. I usually allow myself 2 to 4 meals a week where I break the guidelines and "party". This may include an outrageous dessert, some wine (8 oz.) or an entrée with an outrageous sensual appeal. The other 17 to 19 meals per week, I am a ten. When I go on vacation, I might loosen up even a teeny bit more (and I pay for it) but I get back on track one or two days before I return to normal daily life. My energy levels return and I am ready for the every day challenges we all have to face.

Plan for Diet Change

WEEK #1—TAKE STOCK

Reread this chapter with pen or pencil in hand. Write down what you need to change.

Write down all that you eat and drink.

Analyze and understand what aspects of your diet are not optimum and why. Usually it is due to some emotional attachments to the non-optimal foods. Write down each diet habit or food and what emotion is attached to each for 21 days. Review this list before you eat anything. You need to become aware of the meaning eating has taken on in your life. Then think of an optimal fuel substitution (Example: I eat a candy or drink a beer to reward myself. Thus I am eating these foods out of these emotional responses. I now remind myself that food is not emotional. Food is fuel for my body so instead I will substitute a piece of fruit and a non-alcoholic beverage). This is the discipline part of the formula. (PS it helps to get all emotional foods off your kitchen shelves and replace them with proper fuels)

In three weeks you will think differently about food and you can throw your list away. In the mean time "tough it out" for three weeks. Get committed. It will be worth the effort!

WEEK #2

Start eating 5-6 meals/day. Make meals 2 and 4 snacks. You should never feel full. If you wish you can refer to the calorie charts at the end of the chapter and divide the calories equally into six meals.

Increase fruit intake—have at least one fresh fruit with every meal or snack. (This works well with your method of substituting good "carbs" for bad.)

WEEK #3

Add a salad at lunch and dinner. I almost always have a salad with chicken, lean steak or fish for lunch.

Try adding or substituting one fresh veggie for french fries when out to dinner.

WEEK #4

Evaluate processed foods in your diet. After your diet consists of 70% fruits, veggies, and grains you may eat whatever you want. But, it would be even better if you stayed on the outer aisles of the supermarket, eating only non-processed, organic foods. While this is not a must, you will get better results by minimizing processed meats and processed, boxed and bottled foods.

WEEK #5

Start to increase water intake. This is essential!

Decrease or eliminate carbonated beverages (we are talking soda here). These beverages are comparable to pouring battery acid into your system. They also create bone calcium loss. Consider them a Saturday night treat—not a daily fluid. Decrease or eliminate other, non-optimum, beverages. This includes everything other than water. Drink milk <u>only</u> as a between meal meal. Milk is a complete food designed to be drank by itself and is okay if you are following the entire Power Health Formula. You should restrict your intake of non-optimal fluids to a moderate amount. Coffee for example should be limited to 1 to 2 cups per week.

WEEK #6

Review how you are doing. You should be feeling like a different person by now. Treat yourself, go out and party. Eat and drink whatever and as much as you want. Then see how you feel. You probably feel bloated, stuffed and woozy. Once you prove to yourself that your old diet is killing you, you are ready for week seven.

WEEK #7

Refine and simplify your in between meal snacks. My favorites are dried fruits, nuts, seeds, fruit (of course) with a small chunk of low fat cheese, and chicken or turkey on whole wheat bread.

WEEK #8

Congratulate yourself on a job well done. If you do nothing else in the Power Health Formula you will have reduced your risk of stroke, cardiovascular disease and cancer by at least 50%, if not more, by following the above recommendations.

In case you didn't notice, there are no seven day diet plans or special dishes in this chapter. Now you know why. It is too complicated. I remember one dietary plan.

As you have probably realized by now eating is largely a mindset. Get the mindset. It is all you will ever need to do!

In summary your body has evolved relative to specific universal laws. Among these laws are laws specific to food. Food is your bodies fuel and your body requires you to ingest the appropriate foods and to eliminate of greatly restrict the rest. Food is fuel—food is not emotion or anything else.

Recommendations for optimum fuel intake.

Keep your food journal for three weeks. Get real clear on what you are eating and why you are eating it.

70% veggies, fruits, and grains—eyeball your plate. 70% of what you see should be veggies (salads), fruits, and or grains (breads).

Protein—don't need a ton, but you need it. Keep serving size to the size of your palm per meal. Don't stress over red meat, eggs, cheese or milk but keep them moderate relative to veggies fruits and grains.

Fats—if your eating meat your getting most of the fat you need. If you wish to add fat 1 pad of real butter or one tablespoon of olive oil is plenty per meal.

Eat 5-6 small meals per day. This is easy if you keep the small meals simple (i.e. a few pieces of dried fruit and a piece of cheese—see snack section). These also keep you from hunger pangs and moderate your blood sugar. Meals 1, 3, and 5 are main meals and can range from 500-700 calories, (or eat until full). In between meals (2, 4, and 6 if you choose) are 200-300 calorie snacks. These are not eat until full meals.

Ideally caffeine, alcohol, nicotine, and processed white sugar should be eliminated from your diet. I don't care what any research study says—these substances in combination cause stress, anxiety, nervousness, depression, and oxidation of the cells (better known as aging) and rob you of the vitamins and minerals that the "research" tells you you can't get from your food. You do need salt and sugar but you will get plenty of the right kinds and amounts from your diet. If you must, limit caffinated beverages and alcohol (either separate or in combination) to two cups per day.

Drink tons of water 8-10 glasses/day. Limit fruit juices to one or two glasses/day. Herb teas count as water. <u>Eliminate carbonated soda beverages</u> or at least reduce to 2 cans/glasses per week.

If you are not following the entire Power Health Formula consider a multi vitamin/mineral complex at least until you are with the entire program.

You should be eating 35-42 small meals per week. Don't be perfect 100% of the time. Follow the program 80% of the time. Enjoy yourself the rest. Don't stress you will be fine.

Additional Fuel Components
Oxygen and Breathing

You can only live a few minutes without breathing oxygen but, as with most things, the more abundant they are, the more we take them for granted. We need oxygen. It definitely qualifies as a fuel. But what's the big deal? We all breathe, don't we? Yes and no.

Let us segue to Hawaii for moment. Captain James Cook, the English explorer and navigator, is regarded as having made the first European discovery of Hawaii, first landing at Waimea, Island of Kauai, on January 20, 1778. The early Hawaiians lacked a written language but their culture was entirely oral, rich in myth and legend. Legend has it that upon sighting the pale Europeans, the Hawaiians were immediately struck by the fact that the explorers were chest breathers. In fact they thought it amusing! So amusing that they called the pale people "haolies", which means "men without breath". As descendents of those Europeans, we have inherited their breathing techniques.

We are mostly rank amateurs when it comes to breathing, little leaguers, not even aware that major league breathing exits. Observe your pet when it is resting or asleep. Notice they breathe from their abdomens. You should observe their abdomen—not their chest—expanding and contracting in a long, slow, gentle rhythm. Usually, the longer an animal (and sleeping humans) rest or sleep, the slower

27

and deeper are the abdominal breaths. This brings more oxygen to the cells with less effort.

You need to breathe deeply. It increases your oxygen intake by as much as 60% to 70% and your cells _love_ oxygen. Oxygen is required by every cell in your body to perform its proper metabolic functions and greatly enhances its resistance to disease by helping balance—there's that word again—your immune system. The Chinese consider breathing a science and _the_ most critical element of longevity next to calorie restriction. Breathing in plenty of oxygen brings with it plenty of vital energy. The act of deep diaphragmatic breathing to ingest maximum amounts of oxygen has a multitude of additional physical benefits: aids digestion, decreases indigestion, decreases and corrects most hiatal hernias, aids bowel movements, massages internal organs and glands, purges tissues of toxins (we're talking detoxification again), cleanses the blood stream, stimulates hormone secretions and engages the lymph system and calms you down thus relieving stress.

There are a multitude of illnesses related to simply not using our breathing instrument correctly. Breathe correctly and these illnesses will not occur. The Chinese and Indian traditions have written tomes on the art and science of breathing with a variety of different techniques that are all worth exploring. But my experience with patients has proven to me that by simply committing to breathing from your diaphragm until it becomes a habit will bestow upon you all of the aforementioned benefits and more.

Before getting into diaphragmatic breathing, let's review some more interesting facts about what is probably the most unconscious and taken for granted physiological function of the body. There are two types of breathing. When you stress exhalation you are using the breath to cleanse and detoxify the body. Stressing inhalation collects and stores vital energy. Beginning to sound complicated. It is not. Here is how simple it is. Though you take breathing for granted you already, unconsciously practice both types of breathing spontaneously throughout the day, whenever toxins in the blood stream reach critical levels or when your energy is waning.

I have already told you your body is enough—it knows what to do. Thus, a "sigh" is a spontaneous cleansing breath involving a short inhaling gulp followed by a long, forceful exhalation. By contrast, a yawn is a spontaneous, unconscious energizing breath—a long, slow, <u>deep</u> inhalation, briefly retained in the lungs, followed by a short exhalation. Hmmmmm…Maybe we are not such amateurs after all. The trick is to become more conscious of our breathing so that our natural breathing accomplishes both cleansing and energizing processes with every breath. Here is how.

The Art of Diaphragmatic Breathing

Breathing is a science and an art, particularly in the Orient, where China has its "chee-gung" and India has "pranayama". We have covered many of the positive effects of breathing, but it is beyond the scope of the nature of this book to cover the physiology of breathing and its affects on the body. The beauty is that if you learn the <u>art</u> of breathing, the science will take care of itself, and you will receive all the aforementioned, natural, healthy benefits. So let us examine the art of diaphragmatic breathing.

The difference between the chest breathing Europeans and the deep abdominal breathing Hawaiian natives was the fact that the native deep abdominal breathers had naturally and instinctively learned the role played by the diaphragm in the art of breathing. The diaphragm is a huge muscular structure separating the chest cavity, containing

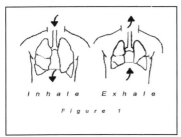

your lungs and heart, from your abdomen containing the rest of your major internal vital organs. When you inhale, the lungs expand and push the diaphragm downward. When you exhale the lungs contract and they pull the diaphragm toward and into the chest cavity (Figure 1).

Western doctors still regard the diaphragm as an unimportant muscle that is only passively involved in breathing. Wrong! But it is not surprising—after all they are chest breathers just like you. Man was meant to breathe primarily with this enormously powerful muscle—not the rib cage. Thanks to laziness, misinformation and ignorance, adults these days invariably become shallow chest breathers rather than the deep abdominal breathers they were meant to be. Chest breathing does <u>not</u> fill the lungs with sufficient amounts of oxygen—ever. As a result you probably take about three times as many chest breaths to get the same amount of air into your lungs as you would receive by a single diaphragmatic breath. Dr. A. Salamanoff describes the function of the diaphragm as follows:

"It is the most powerful muscle in our body; it acts like a perfect force pump, compressing the liver, the spleen, the intestines and stimulating the whole abdominal and portal (liver) circulation.

By compressing the lymphatic and blood vessels of the abdomen, the diaphragm aids the venous circulation from the abdomen towards the thorax (chest cavity, heart and lungs).

The number of movements of the diaphragm per minute is a quarter of those of the heart. But its haemodynamic (blood pumping) power *is much greater* than that of cardiac (heart) contractions because the surface of the force pump (the diaphragm muscle) is much greater and because its propelling power is *superior* to that of the heart. We have only to visualize the surface of the diaphragm to accept the fact that it *acts* like another heart."

Most adults have long ago forgotten how to use their diaphragms to breathe—probably because people do not even know they have such an organ. And even more so because we have become so sedentary and demand less of our physical bodies. Well, now you know. So there is no excuse not to use it.

Here is <u>how</u> to breathe:

FOUR PHASE DIAPHRAGMATIC BREATHING

Inhalation Phase

Relax the abdomen, put your hand on your chest.

Slowly inhale *through the nostrils*, not the mouth, drawing air downward *through* the lungs, *expanding* the diaphragm downward by ballooning the abdomen. The hand on your chest should *not* move and should detect *no* chest motion.

When you think the lungs are full, inhale a little more and then a little more. This fills the middle and top lobes of the lungs.

Never force inhalation beyond your capacity. Your lungs will adapt to comfortable, relaxed inhalations in time. It is not necessary to fill the whole lung every time. Attempting to do this will lead to stress. And The Power Health Formula is <u>not</u> about increasing stress.

Retention Phase

Hesitate a second. Maybe even less than a second. This retains the breath. Even a brief second or two of retention is incredibly cleansing. The retention is incredibly powerful physiologically. Do not worry about the science of what it does. Just do it. You will experience the benefits.

Retain breath no longer than one to three seconds in the beginning use a *gentle closing, "locking"*, of the throat to prevent immediate exhalation, you can eliminate this step later but initially, like focusing on the reason this action focus's you on your breathing. Eventually you will unconsciously eliminate this step.

Dr. Martin P. Rutherford

Exhalation Phase

Exhalation is a more important than inhalation so pay attention.

Previously we used the gentle closing of the throat to stop breath from releasing.

Relax the lock in the throat.

Exhale *gently—through the nostrils* by *compressing your abdomen.* You should *not* feel the hand on your chest move (still have your hand on your chest?). As you increase the force you should feel a strong, *steady* emptying of the lungs *from the bottom to the top.*

At the end of the exhalation pull the abdominal wall (stomach) inward *all the way* without straining. This pushes the diaphragm (remember the diaphragm?) upward towards the chest and empties the air from the lower lungs. This action also compresses the inner organs and empties them of excess blood.

Let abdominal wall relax.

Done!

Breathing Tips

Do not stress or try too hard. Do not make breathing mechanical. Relax. It will come.

Your diaphragm likely has never been used. It is a muscle. It will take time for it to reactivate. Be patient.

Focus on rhythm—not length of breath.

Do this—even if it takes weeks or months—until it becomes self conscious.

There you have it. Never thought you would have to learn to breathe again did you? If you want your organism to operate maximally and if you want Power Health—take the time to learn to breathe. You will be glad you did.

The Science of Breathing

Breathing truly should be regarded as a science. The science covers a great deal more ground than that of the art and is well worth looking into. For instance, debate rages on regarding air pollution - toxic chemicals, smoke from smokestacks, dust from construction and certainly the always present exhaust fumes from tail pipes. It is not the intention of this book to engage in a debate of a political nature, but I think common sense dictates that certainly the better the air quality in which we exist, the more benefits our deep breathing will provide for us. It has long been recognized that when in ideal environments, such as near a lake, in a forest, or next to the ocean you will experience increased energy due to inhaling air which is not only because the air is of a pure clear nature, but because air in mountains and near water is air that contains a much higher ratio of negative ions to positive ions. It has been estimated that the number of negative ions in country air may be five hundred to a thousand times greater than in a polluted city. Why is this so significant?

Because positive ions tend to bring pollutants into our system. Negative ions the good guys enter your body and act much the same way as the antioxidants which we have discussed a number of times in the Power Health CD, book and video series. Negative ions cleanse the body's system by attracting positive ions. Pollutants attach themselves to positive ions. Thus positive ions pollute and "rust" or corrode the body and negative ions attract the positive ions and cleanse them from the body along with attached pollutants. Negative ions by the way are affected negatively by air conditioning and enclosed spaces. They would be negatively affected by central heating and generally by living in apartment like structures which allow little to no exchange between the internal air environment and the external air environment.

This, along with light deprivation, contributes to the exhaustion office workers generally feel by the end of the day. Certainly greater ventilation as well as a healthier air environment would be of great benefit to these individuals. Without getting too crazy or too far out there, I have found that negative ion generators do seem to be of benefit. This has been a controversial issue and an item over the last several years with many of the scientists pooh-poohing it and the alternative movement promoting these machines as the answer. I tend to lean toward the alternative natural health groups in this area. My wife and I have used ion generators ourselves, both in our office as well as in our home, and there is a distinct difference in the air quality. The difference in air quality was noticeable within 24 hours of turning on the machines. After purchasing and installing two ion generators for our almost 4,600 square foot office space, I recall that within 24 hours, our patients were commenting on how clean the air smelled. Those patients that had a great many allergies made comments on the fact that they seemed to be able to tolerate the office air much better because it did not affect their allergies as much or at all.

I do not want to get heavily involved in the debate on clean air. Whether you are living in a clean air environment or whether you are living in a less than optimum clean air environment, breathing more air is still going to be beneficial. Let's stick to the basics of what we are trying to achieve.

Breathing is a technique. It is *not* something that you do naturally. That may sound strange but again, observe. You are probably breathing from your chest at this point. See. Forgot your diaphragmatic breathing lesson already. You should ultimately not only achieve breathing from your abdomen, but you should reach the point where you are speaking from your abdomen as well. Every time you speak you are taking a breath. And every time you take a breath, you want to bring that breath as far into the system as possible. Certainly we speak a lot. So we want to take advantage of the fact that we are speaking. You will find that you have a little deeper voice, maybe, but ultimately you are going to derive great health benefits from this.

To have the motivation to do the work necessary to learn to breathe from your abdomen, it helps to have an understanding as to why we are doing this. It helps to further understand the importance of diaphragmatic breathing and the positive effects it has on the body that chest breathing does not.

More on Diaphragmatic Breathing

Why don't we breathe naturally from the diaphragm? Well, as stated previously, partially we are just plain lazy, but, most of us simply do not understand that there is even a technique to proper breathing or that we should be breathing from the diaphragm. The ignorance of this fact is probably the true reason that no one does so.

There are other reasons why we do not breathe from the diaphragm. Among them are smoking and pollution. Another reason is that folks who have not been breathing from the diaphragm for years have a number of lung problems, which actually prevent them from being physically able to breath from the diaphragm. As a result, of these and other reasons, most of us invariably become chest breathers. As chest breathers we do not pull the air into the lower part of our lungs as efficiently and effectively as we should. This is important because the lower lobes of our lungs are much larger than the higher lobes. The lower lobe of our lungs need and store *more* oxygen than the higher lobes of our lungs. As mentioned in the associated Power Health Audio and Videotapes and CD's, you reduce the number of breaths and the amount of oxygen needed by your system almost 70% by breathing from your diaphragm. You need to use the diaphragm.

Still More Thoughts on Diaphragmatic Breathing

To breathe properly, remember to inhale slowly using the *abdominal muscles* and the diaphragm to draw air into the lungs themselves. In essence, you are really not using the lungs at all to breathe. It is a whole new concept of breathing and if you can change your viewpoint on this matter it will help your breathing technique immeasurably. You are using the diaphragm and abdominal muscles to breathe. The diaphragm will depress as you inhale through the abdomen. You should experience your abdomen <u>expanding</u> and <u>ballooning</u> downward. This is something that people have a difficult time accepting. We are so obsessed with having thin waists and so

35

obsessed with how we look that when we pull our diaphragms down and expand our abdomens we tend to feel that we look silly. It is this very motion that allows opera singers the volume of air intake that is required to pull off the tremendous, forceful high tones and low tones of which they are capable.

When the diaphragm is fully expanded, you are able to fill up the top, middle and lower lobes of your lungs. You can't do this with chest breathing—chest breathing only fils the top lobes of the lungs. At first breathing this way will feel funny. But it is the proper way to breathe. Continue to practice this abdominal expansion. Concentrate on your abdomen. Feel your abdomen expanding. Feel your diaphragm sinking down towards your abdomen. You don't want to feel your chest move at all. In fact, as stated previously, a good way to practice this move is to put your hand on your chest and focus on not feeling your chest moving. You should only feel your *abdomen* expanding and contracting, drawing the air in feeling almost as though you are drawing the air in through your lungs and when exhaling feeling as though you are contracting a bellows, pushing the air out of your nostrils through your lungs with your abdomen.

Start to change your breathing technique today. It will feel odd but stick with it. Breathing correctly is not difficult it just requires some attention. In the beginning your abdomen may not want to expand because of blockages in your intestines or because of weaknesses in a diaphragmatic muscle that has not been used in years. As you continue, you will find it becomes easier and easier. You will gradually achieve a rhythm and experience that you do not need as much effort to breathe as you do now.

If you are interested in delving further into the science and art of breathing, I would refer you to the book, *The Tao of Health, Sex and Longevity*, by Daniel Reid. An entire chapter is devoted to the specifics and the mechanics of diaphragmatic breathing. But in the spirit of this book, I exhort you not to overwhelm yourself with information, not to overwhelm yourself with intricacies but simply to learn to breathe from your diaphragm.

Keep it simple!

Learn to breathe from your diaphragm. As you make advances in breathing from your diaphragm you will experience enough of a change in your health, energy and stress levels to more than motivate you to continue to practice this discipline.

So breathe deep, breathe often, breath from the diaphragm and you will be more likely to continue breathing for a long, long time.

Breathing gives the body the energy it needs for healing by regulating the immune system. It cleanses and it energizes. It reduces stress. It detoxifies the body by detoxifying the blood and improving bowel movements. Breathing energizes by supplying vital building blocks of energy to the cells.

Tips for Helping You Breathe Better

Exercise. Exercising naturally helps you to breathe and oxygenate your entire body.

Walk for twenty minutes. (While breathing from your diaphragm)

Diaphragmatic breathing is essential. Practice breathing from your abdomen.

Quit smoking.

Get a book on breathing exercises.

Additional Fuel Components
Water—H$_2$0

"Water, water everywhere, but not a drop to drink."
Author Unknown

Water is another one of those substances that we take for granted. Our unknown author probably realized that as he was stranded in the middle of the ocean, craving a sip of the essence of life. It would certainly seem ironic to be in the middle of an ocean of water and not be able to partake of any of it. Even on land it would not take very long to realize that you need water to survive once your access to it had been cut off. Yet we take water and its importance to not only our survival but to our health, for granted. Consequently we do not drink enough of it. The standard recommendation for drinking water is to drink approximately 8 eight-ounce glasses of water per day. That is probably not enough.

In interviewing my patients, it was shocking to find that many people drink absolutely <u>zero</u> glasses of water in a day. I'm talking water not carbonated drinks, caffeine, tea, soda, or beer. Though all of these beverages do contain water, these beverages do not count towards the recommended eight glasses a day. A little of this here, a little of that there, maybe a cup of coffee in the morning or a beer a couple of times a week is not going to hurt you as long as you do not overdo them. But for proper fluid fuel intake you need to drink a minimum of eight glasses of *water* a day. It fascinates me that while the body is approximately 75% to 80% water, 99% of all molecules of the body contain water and 85% of the volume of the brain is water most of us refuse to acknowledge the importance of water intake or give it the weight in our health care programs that it deserves.

Would you like to live to a healthy and ripe old age without suffering from headaches, migraines, arthritis, asthma, allergies, diabetes, osteoporosis, stomach pains and a lot of other modern ills? Well, then just turn on your tap. Drinking an abundance of the body's only proper fluid fuel will keep all the body's systems in good working order.

Lack of water severely affects not only the body but also the brain. Lack of water causes depression, it causes stress and anxiety as well as physical diseases. The human body is composed of 25% solid matter and 75% water. When we starve the body's cells of water, they complain in response to dehydration and they set up a multitude of adverse reactions designed to alert us to their needs through these and other related symptoms.

Dr. F. Batmanghelidj M. D., who has authored the book, _Your Body's Many Cries for Water_, says, "When you do not provide your system with the appropriate amount of daily water intake, blood vessels constrict and joints become dry and painful. I believe that stomach pains are almost always a signal that the body is suffering from severe thirst. 50 million Americans suffer from rheumatoid arthritis and another 30 million from lower back pain. I have become convinced that dehydration eventually causes severe damage to joint surfaces."

As a chiropractor, I treat damaged joint surfaces and dry dehydrated discs every day. Those discs are dehydrated due to the fact that the patient is lacking in two aspects of the Power Health Formula. First, they are not getting enough exercise. Exercise pumps fluids into the spinal disc keeping it healthy. Secondly, because they are not drinking the required quantity of water, there isn't enough available to pump into the disc, even if they were getting proper exercise.

Want to avoid a trip to the chiropractor? Exercise. Drink water. It is all too simple.

Think about it. When you were in the womb, you were surrounded by water. You recognized the thirst signals that cried out when you needed liquid and it was not a problem then. That was because you did not have the intellect to think about it. Oh yeah, and you didn't drink. Nature just followed its natural evolution and you received the water that you needed, from mom.

Then you were born and started to grow. Drinking water was *not* natural. You were probably fed formulas, juices and even carbonated drinks to satisfy your needs and to keep you from crying. You become unused to drinking water almost from day one. You lose sensitivity to the need for water before you ever develop it. You are not sensitive to the signals that tell you need *water*, and your thirst signals start to get screwed up.

As we continue to grow and experience thirst, what do we as children learn to drink from society? We learn to drink sodas, colas and juices instead of water. This is the problem. We need to satisfy our thirst with water. We were never taught this simple fact. Most adults do not drink water. Most adults drink tea, coffee and adult drinks. Why? Because we never learned the need for pure 100% unadulterated H_2O in regard to our health.

Why don't I want you to include these beverages in your 8 glasses of water per day? Because they *dehydrate* your body. They dehydrate your body as surely as taking a diuretic water pill. So what are you getting by drinking lots of coffee and tea and beer and alcohol? Just the opposite of what you're trying to achieve. You leach water *out* of your body while thinking you are consuming appropriate fluid intake. And speaking of thinking it has also been shown through numerous experimentations that water probably regulates the subtle energy fields of your body. Science has further considered that the mind body connection probably connects through the subtle energy fields located in the water in the cells of your system. So lack of water probably decreases your ability to utilize the mind/body technique discussed later in the Power Health Formula. So let's get clear. The only fluid the body <u>ever</u> *needs* is water. All other fluids should *not* be regarded as fuels and be used sparingly.

So what *types* of water should you drink? This is one of most controversial issues discussed on my weekly radio program. Should we be drinking bottled water? Should we be drinking chlorinated water? Should we have fluoride in our system or should we not to have fluoride in our system? The debate rages on. In my opinion, all the controversy accomplishes is to add to the amount of health misinformation and confusion that paralyses us and out of frustration, gives us the justification to replace the ever essential water with coffee, tea, soda, beer and wine.

I believe that your water should not have to be bottled water but should come straight out of the tap.

Why?

Because the problem that arises from drinking only bottled water is that if we run out, we intellectually consider that we have no water in the house. It is true. The availability of bottled water has made people forget that there is perfectly drinkable water in our tap. Better yet, it is *freely* available. Yes, tap water usually contains chlorine, an antibacterial agent. But I would not worry about the chlorine in the body as it does not seem to manifest in any great, long term diseases—at least none that I have ever observed. And if you are following the Power Health Formula in its entirety, you will be continually triggering your body's natural detoxification mechanisms, minimizing any potential negative effects.

There is also calcium in tap water. Not to worry. Follow the Formula and the calcium in tap water, along with exercise, will act like as a good protection against osteoporosis. So drink water, in all forms. But learn to love the tap.

Benefits of Proper Hydration

The benefits of drinking water for your system are endless. Water boosts your endurance. Water lessens the amount of carbohydrates that you use as you are exercising. (Weight loss!)

Carbohydrates are what your muscles use for energy. But if you use *too* many "carbs" during exercise, the excess turns to fat. Weird, huh? So do not use sports drinks. Use water.

There have been studies conducted at Baylor College of Medicine indicating that if you are dehydrated, you get sick more often. Another study concludes—drink water to disengage the mucous that coats your throat. Why? Because the mucous helps to trap cold viruses. Guess what? More water, less colds. Got a fever? Start drinking water. Lots of water. The yuckiness you feel when you have a fever, as you lay in bed perspiring, feeling lousy, is because that perspiration is dehydrating your body and your brain. Remember that your brain is 85% water. So if you have the flu, start drinking tons of water. You will feel much better almost immediately.

Water helps headaches. Sufficient water intake helps jet lag. Proper hydration unquestionably, helps improve concentration and reaction time. It has even been proven that if you have a hangover, you are dehydrated. Hung over? Hope not. But if you are, do not start taking painkillers, start drinking water. How much? About 2 ½ quarts every 24 hours after you have had too much too drink. Hopefully, this doesn't apply to you on a frequent basis.

The point here is water. Water is the key.

But Doc, I Cannot Drink That Much Water A Day

How do you get those 64 ounces of water down into each day? I have studied many systems of water intake. Drink this half an hour before you eat. Drink that two hours after you eat. Do not drink this while you eat, do drink that while you are eating. Drink this before you go to bed, don't drink that before you go to bed.

Let's not make this difficult. I have found it to be very simple. I *do* drink enough water. Here's how. I *do not* put myself on a strict routine. When I get up in the morning, the very first thing I do is grab a warm glass of water. The reason it is warm is because I have found that drinking warm water first thing in the morning stimulates the bowels. Most days I will get out of bed, walk straight to the tap and pour a glass of warm tap water. This first drink starts to engage my thirst mechanism and makes me aware of my body's water balance. Generally by the time I am out of house, I have leisurely drunk another glass of water or two while going about my morning business.

I do carry bottled water with me in the car. I might drink from it. I might not. But it is there. From this point in time, until the end of the day, I tend to continually sip. So the first two glasses of water I have in the morning, I carry around the house with me. They are indeed tap water and I sip them.

Tip: <u>Do</u> <u>not</u> chug your water! It will fill you up and bloat you. It will discourage you from drinking any more. Many of the people who claim they cannot drink *that much water* are the people who get a glass of water and try to drink it all at once. This is not the way to do it.

Now I am on my way to work, maybe sipping a bottle of water. When I get to work, I get three glasses of water and I put them at my workstations. These are the areas where I interview people, where I take histories and where I manipulate their spines, do massage therapy and whatever they require. As I am speaking to them, no one seems to be offended if I pick up that glass of water and sip it. I do this throughout the day.

I will generally sip 3 to 5 six ounce glasses of water on my morning shift which ends at 12:30 p.m. Then I go to lunch. At lunch I might have some tea, which I do not count as my water. When I come back to my office, I refill my glasses with water. I continue to sip. No system. I just sip. In sipping the water all day, I do not have any sense of fullness, and it gives me quite a bit of energy and clarity of mind.

By five or six o'clock at night, I have usually consumed more than enough water to meet my body's requirements. This leaves me free to enjoy whatever type of beverage I would like in the evening. The question is: how do I drink this amount of water and not end up in the bathroom all the time? Answer: in the beginning you <u>will</u> end up in the bathroom a lot. This is okay. Actually, this is preferable. When urinating, you will be looking for a clear stream of urine. When I say clear, it should match the clarity of the water in the toilet bowl.

Once you have observed that clarity (it might take a few days or more), you can be assured that your body is cleansing and detoxifying. As you continue to drink the amount of water that your body requires, you will become very sensitive to the amount that your body requires. This awareness is a process that takes weeks, and maybe even months to develop. Your body's detoxification system (which includes your skin perspiring, your kidneys urinating, and your breath exhaling toxins, just to name a few) will regulate to the amount of water that you are consuming. Your kidneys will ultimately regulate to the degree that you will not find yourself running for the bathroom any more than you are today. So you will experience a period of highly increased urinary output, but you will come back to "normal", even drinking 8 or 9 eight ounce glasses of water per day.

Please understand how important water is to your system, and that you cannot put enough water in your body through any method other than drinking plenty of it!

One last point on water. Initially your thirst is not an appropriate gauge for how much water to drink. Your current thirst is gauged to the amount of water you are *presently* putting in your system. You must set a goal of drinking a minimum of 8 eight-ounce glasses of water a day. Your thirst gauge may become more accurate after weeks or months of appropriate water intake but initially will not be a gauge as to how much water you really need.

Remember when water is plentiful, it positively affects every cell and all physiological processes. Water improves your blood viscosity, your joint cartilage, your digestive system, your blood capillaries, your hydroelectric system, and the health of your spinal column. All systems work in an easy, efficient manner when your body has enough water. When the water supply becomes scarce, the body robs some systems of fluid, rerouting these fluids to other less hydrated systems to assure that other areas of your body have enough that were being deprived of water. This action results in pain and, eventually, in tissue damage.

The body always responds to insufficient water with *emergency measures*. Your body is not designed to live in a constant state of emergency. Understand dehydration and its dire consequences on your health. Sufficient daily water intake is the only solution. It is so simple.

Dr. Martin P. Rutherford

Additional Fuel Components
Light

"I see the light."

You know, we see the light. Light, like oxygen and water, seems to be taken for granted these days. That which we do not have to work for and which is supplied in abundant quantities has little meaning to us. But our bodies have evolved as light absorbing organisms. Like all organisms, human beings are sensitive to light. Light sensitivity is not a passive phenomenon. It is a part of our biological cycle as part of nature. In order to optimally maintain our light sensing mechanisms (i.e. eyes and skin), we have to absorb light. How do we better absorb light? By getting that light absorbing mechanism in our body working optimally. So in accordance with our Power Health Formula, we need to ingest those optimum fuels for these organs like carrots and water. Oh, fruits and vegetables, there you go again. They keep popping up everywhere we go.

Foods containing vitamin A enable the eye pigment to absorb light by replenishing the supply of rhodopsin and other light sensitive chemicals in the retina and water keeps the skin sensitive.

One of the most important reasons our bodies need to absorb light is to see. Let's talk about sight for a moment. Light travels in straight

46

lines at 186,000 miles per second until it hits something. Hopefully one of the things that it hits is going to more and more frequently be your body. Light rays are then reflected off of whatever they hit. You, the houses next door, someone else's face, the tree, whatever. Or the rays may penetrate a new medium. For example, into water, or a glass or your cornea. Then these rays are slowed down and bent. In other words, they are refracted. The refraction slows them. It is this bending of rays hitting your <u>healthy</u> retina (because you are eating your veggies and drinking your water) that makes the images that allows you to see. Seeing is a good thing.

The convex cornea and the convex lenses in your eye bend these lights to focus. Light rays reflected from close objects (such as the words on this page) diverge. This is not good for sight because we need these rays to <u>converge</u> so the cornea needs help from the lens to converge light rays and get a sharp image. Unlike a lens of a camera, which moves back and forth to focus, the lens of the eye changes shape. The lens changes shape and flattens to focus on distant objects. If it needs to focus on objects that are close up, the lens becomes thicker and rounder. In fact, close up work becomes difficult as people age because the lens, like other parts of the body, has lost <u>moisture</u> and elasticity.

Why does it lose moisture and elasticity? Because of old age? No, not really. <u>Because we do not drink enough water</u>. Remember water? Oh, yes. And we do not exercise our eyes enough. Yes, that's right—exercise.

You need to exercise those eyeball muscles by getting out of the house or office and doing activities that require sight. (walking will do) Our eyes are transformers. They sense light around us and they turn that light into electrical impulses that the brain can interpret. The eye is designed to handle its own medium. It admits light waves, bends them at the cornea and the lens, as discussed earlier, and then focuses the waves on the retina. Ultimately, they send their signals to the brain via the nervous system, which we will talk about in the integrated highway aspect of the Power Health Formula. Thus light ultimately produces vision in us.

So how do we keep this mechanism optimally working? That's right—get outside into the light, often.

Light goes way beyond producing vision. Light helps your metabolism. Light enables your body to metabolize vitamin D and calcium. Health experts are advising you daily to take vitamin D and calcium. And, for what? To prevent osteoporosis. Vitamin D is produced in the skin. And from exposure to what? Sunlight. It is argued that this production declines with age. I do not believe that. I contend that it declines because people do not exercise enough, that people do not get out into the sunlight enough and that people decline eating the optimum fuels for calcium metabolism—veggies, veggies, veggies!

Without enough light, you cannot have a sufficient level of vitamin D and calcium, period. So your doctors are continually telling you to take 400 to 800 international units of vitamin D and 1200 milligrams of calcium. Why? To reduce the incidences of hip fractures. This works. Increasing calcium reduces hip fractures by as much as 43%. Now wouldn't you want to do that without having to take thousands of supplements? Wouldn't you want to have strong bones and an appropriate amount of vitamin D, inexpensively and on your own power? Of course you would.

Remember—you and your body are enough. And look at how simple it is. Get enough exercise, eat right, and get enough sunlight. (We will get to the mind/body connection later)

There are even more benefits to absorbing sufficient light. Light affects sleep patterns. Our biological clock and its rhythms are regulated by exposure to light. Daylight tells your body, through the pineal gland, to stop secreting melatonin. Surely you have heard of the hormone melatonin. Entire books have been written on supplementing with this natural hormone. As a hormone, it can function to depress you as well as to induce sleep. Too much melatonin and you will be in a continuing state of tiredness or even depression. The melatonin regulating mechanism alone is enough of a reason to get outside and see the light.

It is always amazing to me how many of us never go outside. Ever! We get up in the morning and get ready for work, often in the darkness. Much of the time, often times, we drive to work in total darkness. We get to the office, and frequently occupy an enclosed artificially lighted environment which not only affects the quality of the air we breath but the quality and quantity of light absorbed by our system. In addition to the above-described workplace scenario the majority of the human population does not get exercise and a large percentage of those who do exercise, never go outside, instead making the trek to the gym. It is not an unusual situation to see people whose only light absorption during a day occurs while walking to and from their car.

Light is not an option.

Einstein discovered that light is as physically solid and as real an element as the food, oxygen and water already discussed as so vital to the functioning of your body. And it is equally important as an element of our health. Yet light has become the bad guy. Every year we, prior to the summer sun season, are inundated with warnings regarding the sun, light rays, skin cancer, sunscreens, sunburns, sun everything. Sun hats, sunglasses and whatever else that will scare you and keep you from going into the sun are maligned as the bad guys. The ozone layer controversy has only added to our fear of the natural and the bad rap on sunlight.

Sunlight is not a bad guy. Sunlight is a good guy. Like the other natural elements, all are beneficial when taken in moderation and in balance. Remember balance? Please do not ever forget that!

So, how do I get sun? Simple again. I go outside every chance that I get. *Every* chance I get. On my off days, I make certain to take walks or jog once or twice a day. On other days (i.e. work days), I do a number of things in order to get enough sunlight entering my corneas so it can get into my system and do all the good things that my body needs it to do.

First of all, I rarely use sunglasses. Controversial, but I have found it extremely beneficial. I wear sunglasses only when I believe I am going to be exposed to direct sunlight for a long period of time. You get more than enough protection from the sun. When walking outside, very few people walk facing the sun. Most of us walk with our heads straight forward and those furrowed eyebrows of ours along with our eyelids to a good job of blocking enough sun, to keep that appropriate amount of sunlight coming into our eyes without burning them. So when I get into the car to travel to work or wherever, I put my sun glasses next to me, but I do not put them on. Between sun visors, tinted glass and the angle of the glass, you get more than enough protection from your vehicle as you are driving.

I live in a mountainous area. Often times I drive into sunsets or sunrises. If my eye contact is in the direct line of sunrays or looking directly at the sun, I will then don my sunglasses for the amount of time necessary to be able to see well, drive safely and not damage my retina. I might even use my hand to block out sunrays. But when I am no longer looking directly into the sun's rays I take my sunglasses off.

The best way to get sufficient sunlight is to exercise outside. I utilize a gym environment to exercise. But several times a week, I get outside and take a short run, hike, jog or a walk. I only use treadmills and stationary bikes when there are blinding snowstorms outside. It is better to get outside and experience the sun. On workdays, when I have been inside for a long time, I take at least five minutes during lunch and walk outside in the parking lot behind my office. During this short walk, I look up to the sky, not directly at the sun, but toward the sky. This action bathes my skin and my eyes in sunlight, getting that all-important photosensitivity reaction from my eyes and skin. This seemingly trivial action starts the process of vitamin D being manufactured and leading to a proper manufacturing and modulating of my calcium content. It also energizes me for the work I face during the afternoon hours of my workday.

There isn't a whole lot more to be said about sun and getting sunlight. Do not be afraid of the sunlight. Skin cancers are caused by <u>overuse</u> and <u>overexposure</u>. Anybody who lays out in the sun two to three hours a day for the entire summer or summers, sunburn after sunburn after sunburn is going to be exposing themselves to a higher risk of skin cancer, no argument here. But following the Power Health Formula in its entirety dictates <u>balance</u> and is not going to increase your risk of eye problems or skin cancers to any measurable degree whatsoever. As a matter of fact, the sunlight exposures recommended above can only be beneficial.

So I hereby declare war on all those that have made light the bad guy. Light is not a bad guy, light is your friend. Learn to like it. Make it a habit to get out into it. Learn to enjoy it. You will be the healthier for it.

Light Factoids

Direct sunlight improves brain function. Prolonged lack of light causes depression.

Full spectrum light is necessary to stimulate the pituitary and pineal glands. The pineal gland is the gland that produces melatonin. Melatonin puts us to sleep; it depresses us. Don't want to be depressed, do we? Lobby to get full spectrum lighting in your work place. It is worth the hassle and expense.

You need quality sunlight. Quality sunlight means full spectrum, ultraviolet light, better know as the sun.

Lack of solar radiation negatively affects the nervous system and causes vitamin D deficiency. This weakens the immune system and affects chronic bone disease. Another good treatment for arthritis. Sunlight.

All windows reduce sunlight. Sunglasses are okay, but they filter out the most important rays and that being the ultra violet rays. Can the designer glasses, except in obvious situations (glare, skiing, on the water, etc.) and save yourself beaucoup bucks.

51

Rules for Getting Good Sunlight

Get daily exposure of naked skin and bare eyes to the sun for at least five minutes. Take your shirt off if necessary, guys. Gals, get plenty of sun on your arms, neck, face and on your legs. But try to get exposure on your skin as well as your eyes.

When indoors for too long, take a walk. Get outside. Get out of the artificial light.

Consider purchasing full spectrum light, this will increase your energy if you are indoors all the time.

Watch T. V. as little as possible or not at all. Its radiation has negative affects on your body. And I could write a book on what the content does to your mental attitude.

Get rid of sunglasses. Or at the very least, use them more judiciously.

Interconnected Highways

Interconnected highways refers specifically to the nervous system and indirectly to the structure and function of the bones, muscles, cartilage, tendons, ligaments and all of the supporting structures of our body. In my experience, this is the least understood aspect of all health care formulas.

People come to my office and ask me, "How did I get this problem?" "Why is my back hurting?" "How could my middle back be out of place?" "Why do I have a neck pain shooting down into my arm? I did not do anything." "Why are my feet flat?" "Why are my knees bothering me?" "I did not have an accident. I haven't fallen. I haven't injured myself. I haven't lifted anything. All of a sudden it just started to hurt."

It astonishes me that we spend so much time staring into the mirror rather than trying to grasp the fundamental, general concepts of our physical and structural body. Without these concepts, we are doomed to poor health and enormous frustration with a medical system that also does not understand the simple, basic mechanics of the body. Most of the common ailments of "old age" are really the cumulative effects of our environment (particularly gravity) as well as physical and emotional stress on our bones and all our body's supporting structures.

What we refer to as "old age" is simply the cumulative shrinking and compression of the body's soft tissues, all of the structures mentioned above, minus the bones. Ultimately this affects not only our organs, our joints and our external appearance but, most importantly, our nervous system.

Structure and function are buzzwords in the body working field today. What they mean is very simple. Your structure should be functioning. If you have found your way into my office, a physical therapist's office, an orthopedics office, a massage therapist's office, a rolfer's office or any other of the numerous body workers available in the field today, I can promise you, your structure is not functioning.

What do I mean by that? Your body is composed of a number of hard and soft tissues. The hard tissues of your body are your bones, of which you have 206. The soft tissues, numbering in the hundreds, are everything else: muscles, ligaments, tendons, organs, nerve tissue, etc. These tissues are intricately inter-related and designed to function synergistically. When these tissues work in harmony your body can be healthy. Harmony includes the efficient movement of all your body's hard and soft tissues as well as the exchange of all of the fluids in your body.

There are a number of body-work disciplines (i.e. Raiche, Chi Kung, etc.) that have appeared on the scene today, each claiming their success results from removing energy blockages and allowing the energy to flow freely through your body. This may seem rather esoteric and many times difficult to understand. But, to a great extent, their claims are true: you need energy flowing to all areas of the body. That can only occur if all of the structures in your body are physically moving freely.

Each joint in your body, your shoulders, your knee joints, your wrist joints and your ankle joints should move freely and individually. When these joints are moving, they allow the muscles to move freely and individually. Muscles that are not damaged should have a full range of motion.

Consider the vertebrae in your spine they number 24. Each vertebra should move freely and individually. When the spinal muscles and the bones are moving properly, they keep pressure off of the nerves exiting from between the bones in your spine.

Properly functioning structures allow fluids to pass freely around joints and not back up, as in people with swollen ankles or calves. Fully functioning joints allow lymph fluids, part of your body's detoxification mechanism, to flow freely. Fully functioning joints allow the bodily fluids to pass into and out of all of your organs unimpeded, enabling the body to experience the maximum nutritional benefits and detoxification.

Lastly, all of this free movement in the bones, muscles and organs allows a proper flow of energy. So having properly integrated communication highways includes free flow of the physical and spiritually (non-physical) electrical components of your systems. Again, the body has it all. It is totally designed to function on its own, if you just keep everything moving.

Every cell in your body needs a nerve supply and proper nutrition. Having a properly functioning nervous system is critical to achieving an optimally functioning body. The nerve supply emanates from your brain. The electrical impulses generated in your brain travel down your spinal cord at 270 mph. They then travel out the nerves that go to all of your organ tissue and every cell in your body. These nerve impulses ride the nervous system's integrated highway. They carry the all-important electrical supply throughout the body, allowing each cell to be alive and achieve its optimal metabolism and function.

Likewise, every cell in your body needs fuel—proper nutrition. Every cell in your body gets that fuel through either a direct feed from your arterial/venous system or through a process called imbibition in which nutrients are supplied to tissues through *motion* of the joint, forcing fluid into the tissue. Forcing nutrient fluids into tissue and toxic fluids out of tissue are two essential processes that every cell in your body requires to function. Cells receive fuel from the blood system and electrical impulses through the integrated nerve highway.

Harmony exists if your body's structure and function allows cells to receive these vital components.

Why wouldn't your body's structure and function allow free flow of nerve supply and/or the free flow of body fluids that nourish and detoxify your system?

The most obvious reason is that the body becomes injured and destroys tissues. Repair of the injured tissues results in formation of adhesions and scar tissue, contributing to restricted function and movement of the injured part. If we get a severe leg injury, frequently it swells because the blood supply cannot flow freely. That is relatively easy for us to understand.

If we get an injury to our neck, irritating a nerve and causing a pain to shoot down into our arm or an injury to our lower back, damaging a nerve causing the pain to shoot down into our leg, we call these "pinched nerves". Again we seem to understand this phenomenon pretty well. Injuries and subsequent tissue damage obviously interfere with proper functioning of the body.

But there are other forces that subtly rob our body of its ability to function normally. It is the very subtlety of these forces and their gradual, almost unnoticeable change in our bodies, our quality of life, which makes it so important to become aware of these intruders and to understand how to overcome them. It is to these issues that I address this chapter.

Gravity—the greatest cause of wear and tear on the structure of your body—is another one of those things that we have taken for granted since Newton discovered it God knows how many years ago. You do not see gravity; it is invisible; you cannot touch it; you cannot taste it; you cannot smell it. But, lose your footing and fall and you will become aware of just how forcefully gravity sucks us down to the ground. Though gravity is a constant, powerful influence on our physical bodies, we rarely think about gravity and that it has any influence whatsoever over our mental or physical well being.

As human beings we are a pretty egocentric group. We tend to believe we are the center of the universe and that everything revolves around us. One of the points I intend to drive home with the Power Health Formula is that we are indeed *a part of nature*, not separate from it, and if we can get back to the basics of how to operate within the natural law we, as a population, can cut our sickness and disease rates by at least 85% to 90%.

I believe ignorance and egocentricity cause us to not live within natural law and not get back to nature. We do not *feel* a part of nature. We feel apart from nature. We view ourselves as separate from and above nature. If you feel this way you must abandon this belief. It is destroying your chance to achieve true health. Like it or not, we are part of nature and bound by her laws.

Gravity is part of nature. Gravity continually and forcefully exerts its downward pull on our body's physical structure. We live in a sea of gravity and must realize that existing in this earth environment requires that we to learn to deal with the constant, cumulative effects of gravity. For example, when we fall as mentioned above, we believe we fall. We actually use the term "fall" to mean that I am in control, I lose control, and I "fall" to the ground. When we walk every step we take is the performance of a balancing act against gravity. Gravity supplies resistance but also the impetus that allows you to walk and run. We are balancing ourselves against gravity at all times. When we lose that balance, *gravity* sucks *us* down and slams *us* into the earth. Falling is losing control to gravity.

Once you understand this basic concept, you understand better why, over a period of time, our faces, our necks, our shoulders, our chests and our backs start to sag and why we lose the tone of our muscles. A great many of the ills and woes that we attribute to old age simply result from failing to acknowledge and deal with the effects of gravity on the structure and functions of our body.

Gravity is always there. Twenty-four hours a day, seven days a week, 365 days a year. It is there from youth to old age.

Gravity has a tremendous effect on every function of your body. It can prevent the flow of blood from your legs back up to the heart and into your head, as well as cause structural damage in the spine such as degenerated discs. If you need more proof of gravity's profound and constant stress on your body, lie down in bed and stay there for a week. All of your bodily fluids will "pool" and your soft tissues (skin, fat, muscles) will actually conform to the shape of the bed. Gravity is powerful. It is always there.

Gravity is probably the number one reason for joint problems and poor circulation. Understand this fact and it should become obvious that by not strengthening your muscular system and by not keeping in motion, (which we will discuss shortly) you lose control to gravity. The medical profession usually attributes these conditions to "old age". It is not old age. It is cumulative trauma, cumulative stress, and cumulative gravity.

Let's talk about posture relative to gravity. I am 50 years old at the time of the publishing of this book, and I am sure you as well as I can remember, our parents admonishing us to stand up straight. It was one of the mantras of their age group. If you are like me, I thought it was just one more thing my parents used just to harass me. As it turns out, it was good advice. (How old were you when first you realized that your parents gave you at least some good advice?)

Posture is everything. Posture is a big part of *your effort* to combat gravity. Because of gravity, you are continually shrinking. Bummer, huh? But it is inescapable. Our office enjoys considerable success at reversing spinal, knee and ankle conditions. It is because our treatment addresses reversing the effects of gravity through tractioning the spine, decompressing the knees, and taking pressure off the ankles with manipulation, orthodics, and other corrective devices. Posture training is invaluable in the correction of these conditions.

Patients regularly ask, "Why am I in pain?" or "How did I get in this condition?" Usually the patient is relatively stooped over, has poor posture and has pressure on every joint in their body. It is a pressure that has come from a cumulative lifetime of doing nothing to offset or reverse the effects of gravity; or doing nothing to keep their fluids and/or joints moving. So we teach these patients, among other things, good posture.

Good posture has a myriad of benefits relative to the functioning of the body. Good posture allows you to breathe efficiently. Recall the oxygen component of the Power Health Formula. Good posture allows you to more easily perform the suggested diaphragmatic breathing because it allows you much easier access and less resistance to expanding your abdomen. Good posture removes pressure from your spinal joints and all other bodily joints. Good posture allows bodily fluids to flow freely into and out of your tissues.

Conversely, when you are standing or sitting slouched and bent over, you compress the various joints and vital internal organs of the body. Fluids are not allowed free flow in the joints or via the arterial/venous/lymph systems. Fluids get backed up. Joints dry up. The next thing you know, backed up fluids start causing problems which doctors like to put names on (better known as diagnosis) like arthritis, edema, congestive heart failure and then expose you to unnecessary drugs and surgeries.

Good posture, as an integral part of the entire Power Health Formula, prevents these conditions and many more. Good posture allows efficient bowel elimination, by not compressing your abdominal tissues and stopping the flow. Good posture allows you a tremendously increased energy because it enables you to operate more efficiently. Who doesn't need more energy? Suppose your choices are caffeine, ginseng or good posture? I'll take good posture, please. The list of benefits of improved posture goes on and on. It's endless.

Good posture is one of those concepts that has been overdone, but not understood. Our parents and our teachers tell us to do it. But frequently we don't know why's good for us. Posture has been presented to us so often throughout our lifetime that we minimize its importance to our quality of health and life the same way we minimize the importance of the of proper fuels, drinking proper amounts of water, breathing correctly, eating fruits and vegetables, exercising and all of the other components of the Power Health Formula.

Good posture is vital to you living a long, effective and quality life. Stand tall. It matters!

It is up to you. All the elements necessary to achieve abundant health and posture are a part of the Power Health Formula. Just access them.

So relative to maintaining the integrated highways of optimum nerve impulse and fluid flow, how do we achieve proper posture? For those of us not fortunate enough to have had proper posture training when we were children, we need to make a concerted effort to regain this important weapon against gravity and "aging".

Attaining proper posture requires us to get off our butts and get moving!! The number one rule of life is to *keep moving*. When we discuss structure and function of the body, the integrated nerve highways and bodily fluid exchange, we are discussing movement. If you are not, mentally or physically, "too far gone", and most people are not, the easiest way to start to correct your posture is to begin to move - all the time.

Life is movement.

Joints need to be moved to keep healthy fluids in them. Muscles need to be moved to stay supple. Fluids need to be moved through the body. Bodies need to move. It's so simple. Movement is the key. Talk to anyone in their eighties or nineties, vitally healthy and functioning well. They will tell you that one element of their success formula is that they have remained active. They will inevitably tell you that they have kept moving.

Not being a sedentary couch potato, moving your body, is critical to achieving good posture. Without joint movement, you really cannot even begin to improve your posture. Why? Because changing and reshaping your tissues, to a give you a new, taller, upright spinal and bone structure, requires movement.

All of the soft tissues in your body are elastic. They can change shape. Really!! Don't believe it? Observe a pregnant woman. Observe how the abdominal tissues adapt to the affects and the "expansive" changes her body undergoes while carrying a growing fetus. These changes affect muscular, ligamentous, fat and skin tissues. Understanding that your tissues can actually be remodeled and reshaped may help motivate you to take the necessary steps to change your posture.

Here's another example of the fact that we can, with effort, change the shape of the tissues of our bodies. Scoliosis is a lateral curvature of the spine. Severe scoliosis results in hunchback deformities. In our office, we can achieve non-surgical reductions and corrections of scoliosis. How can we reduce abnormal curvatures of the spine without surgery? Seems impossible. But we can do it because the soft tissues of the spine—the muscles, ligaments, tendons, disc tissues—can all be gradually changed if you apply pressure over a long enough period of time.

I repeat that the body's tissues are elastic and can change shape. Understanding this concept is critical. Many people will not even attempt to improve posture because they believe that bad posture cannot be changed. It can be changed. It takes time. And with the proper approach, posture changes gradually, but it can be changed.

So how do we soften up these tissues and improve our posture? There are several relatively fun ways to accomplish this goal. A simple and moderately effective method of reshaping your soft tissues is to start a weight-training program. Commit to a generalized weight program - I am not talking about becoming a body builder. I am talking about a basic weight program that exercises every muscle and every joint in your body two to three times a week. As you progress in your weight resistance training program joints free up, you experience increased strength of the muscular system and increased freedom and function. Increased elasticity in the muscles and increased joint function allow you to stand up straighter.

You do not need a personal trainer. Most gyms will allow you a trial of one free session in which they will demonstrate to you how to use all the weights and which exercises to use for your specific health goals. However, if you can afford a trainer to fine-tune your program, go for it. When people ask me the best way to reduce the need for my (chiropractic) service and to improve posture, I always reply, "Hit the gym!" Movement is life. Never forget that!!

Beyond using a structured weight resistance program for remodeling and restructuring the tissues of the body and improving posture, you should undertake either Tai Chi or Yoga. It is beyond the scope of this book to discuss these disciplines in their entirety. However, both of these "exercise programs" are disciplines that are simple, do not require any equipment, can be done anywhere, can be done without injury and will produce <u>profound</u> changes in posture over time. A weight resistance program or the Home Power Health Video coupled with ten minutes of either Yoga or Tai Chi would constitute the most complete exercise program possible to restructure your posture.

A few words on the Power Health Exercise Video. Exercise is absolutely critical to achieving improved posture and Power Health. Thus we include the "catalyst" of exercise in this chapter on the integrated highway component of the Power Health Formula. As I stated above, life is motion. *If you do not move* you *will* pay the price. Couch potatoing (inactivity) is America's number one health enemy today. It is destroying our health and quality of life. You need not become an Olympic athlete to be healthy. But, you *do need* to move.

It saddens me when I see a seventy five year old patient walk in the door, crouched over and barely able to move, due to tissues that have contracted and shrunk from years of the effects of gravity and traumas. My first thoughts are, "It did not have to be that way—It is not old age—It is lack of movement." Conversely, I treat patients in their eighties and nineties who are runners and skiers and are active in all of life's activities. They kept moving. If there is a Fountain of Youth, exercise is probably it.

Exercise is the catalyst to all elements in the Formula. It improves your body's posture, structure and function. Exercise helps you assimilate your food better. With exercise you utilize oxygen better. Exercise, if done outside, will get you in the sunlight. Exercise usually requires you to ingest more amounts of water. Exercise allows you to break down nutrients and get them to every area of need in your body. People who exercise sleep better. Exercise allows the fluids in your body to move and keeps your joints freed up.

Ok, the benefits of exercise are abundantly clear to most of us. But exercise takes effort (and so does life). To this end, Max McManus, my personal trainer, the owner of Maximum Results Personal Training Center in Reno, Nevada, and I have devised an exercise program that we believe to be an effective component of the Power Health Formula. This exercise program was designed to be simple but powerful. It can be done in twenty minutes and we would encourage you to use this exercise program three to four times a week, preferably every other day. You may use it in place of a full weight resistance training program.

The Power Health Exercise Program allows you to achieve more exercise benefits than you might expect from a program that is mere twenty minutes in length. The program is basic, effective and complete. All you need is a chair, a floor and a wall. It can be done virtually anywhere. Perform the exercises properly and you will receive strengthening, balancing, cardiovascular and flexibility benefits.

If there is a panacea for all ills, exercise comes very close to it. So please take advantage of the Power Health Exercise Video. Order forms are located in the appendix. We have found the Program to be very effective with our patients and it is our answer to "Doc, what do I have to do to stop coming back into your office?"

The body's interconnected highways are kept free flowing by proper structure and function of joints and tissues. The body functions better if your structure is aligned properly and *all* joints are moving freely. Life is motion. You need to have all the joints and all of the muscles in your body moving, allowing the free flow of the nerve supply and fluids in your body.

Good posture is critical and can be achieved. Exercise improves structure, function and posture. So exercise and reverse the effects of

63

gravity. Get the structure functioning properly. Get that interconnected highway and that nervous system sending those signals to every cell in your body and you will experience a significant increase in energy, immunity and well being.

Rest

The "R" in The Power Health Formula stands for rest, better known as sleep. According to the National Commission on Sleep Disorders Research, between 70 and 100 million Americans are sleep deprived or suffer from frequent or chronic insomnia. If you feel you cannot stay awake during afternoon meetings; if you sleep extra hours on weekend mornings; if you are using caffeine to try to give you a boost and keep you alert during the day; if you need to use an alarm to get out of bed you are probably one of them. You are trying to live a life in which you basically feel as though you can never catch up. Being tired negatively affects every aspect of your life, every aspect of your health and every component of the Power Health Formula.

How can you make competent, reliable, critical, personal and business decisions in an impaired state of chronic fatigue? You cannot. That is all there is to it. Yet sleep, another one of those life's basics, nevertheless ends up being a highly controversial issue in this country. Many consider it a badge of honor to garner only four, five, or six hours of sleep a night. If you are one of them, you are in for a rude awakening.

Knowledge about sleep, just like knowledge about exercise and nutrition is essential for your life, happiness, productivity and general health. At a minimum you need to know how much sleep you require. I can tell you right now, four to six hours doesn't cut it.

It is a rare person that can effectively function with six hours of sleep and that person can probably only do that if they are following, in their entirety, the rest of the components of the Power Health Formula. You may be blissfully ignorant of how sleep deprived and ineffective you are during your daily activities. This is particularly true if you are one of the millions of Americans who stays up late watching Dave, Jay, or Conan. Doing that deprives you of vital sleep and you end up trudging through the next day solely on will power. We are about to change that.

How much sleep do you need? If you want to be mentally alert, if you want a good memory, if you want your immune system to function optimally, if you want to be able to do tasks right the first time, you need to sleep at least eight to ten hours a night. That's right, I said *eight to ten hours* each and every night. No, this is not a typo!

If you are not following most of the aspects of the Power Health Formula, I can promise you that a minimum of eight to ten hours of sleep per night is required. Eight to ten glasses of water a day, eight to ten hours of sleep at night.

I can hear it now. "I can't afford the time." "I need more time to unwind." "I am going to miss my favorite shows on television." That is all well and fine if don't care about optimal health! But if you want the self-empowerment, that feeling of clarity and control we are talking about, if you want that energy that makes you five times more efficient than you are today, you will change your priorities and get the appropriate amount of sleep.

Sleep provides tremendous power. Spending that one third of your life in bed positively affects your waking hours. Sleep is simply a part of your existence on this planet. You cannot cheat it or it cheats you. No matter how hard you try, eventually you must sleep.

Lack of sleep reduces your alertness, decreases your energy and makes you irritable. You are not able to remember things or think as clearly. Your reflexes are profoundly slowed and certainly your work productivity is negatively affected by lack of sleep. Want to advance on the job? Want a better relationship? Sleep more, not less.

Your performance, your mood and your creativity all suffer if you do not get enough sleep. And how many people are killed out there everyday because they fell asleep at the wheel? Recent studies have compared driving while sleep-deprived to driving while intoxicated. Believe it or not, poor sleep habits even effect your weight.

Sleep has far-reaching physiological effects. Sleep affects everything. Sleep regulates your digestive system. Sleep regulates heart function and most importantly, relative to the Power Health Formula, sleep profoundly affects your immune function. <u>As much as 60% of the body's disease and wound healing occurs during deep Delta, sleep</u>. Sleep further energizes your body and helps your brain function. The benefits of proper sleep go on and on and on.

Many believe that sleeping wastes valuable time. Nothing could be further from the truth. Sleep is not a passive activity. Sleep is a very, very active endeavor. In fact, there are four distinctly active stages of sleep. Each stage has its own particular function. No function of your body occurs without a specific goal or purpose. The "activity" of sleep is no exception. In truth, sleeping is almost work.

There are four stages of sleep and for optimum health you need to experience all of them, as many times as eight to ten hours of sleep will allow.

In the first stage of sleep your heart rate slows down and stabilizes. Breathing becomes shallow and regular. Remember the breathing component of the Power Health Formula? Shallow, regular diaphragmatic breathing is the breathing technique I would like you to employ during waking hours. Diaphragmatic breathing occurs *naturally* during the first stage of the sleep cycle. Observe another sleeping human being or an animal sleeping and you will see this abdominal breathing.

Also in stage one, skeletal muscles relax. In fact, your muscles relax so quickly in this stage, you might actually jerk yourself awake from the immediate, profound relaxation of your muscular system. How often do you really take the time to relax?

In stage two, a deeper stage of sleep, you continue to experience further reduction of muscular tightness. Anyone out there want stress reduction? Stage two is considered by many researchers to be the actual beginning of sleep. It is in this stage that we begin losing our ability to recognize our environment and we thus become immune to the noises that generally keep us awake.

Stage three sleep is called theta/delta sleep. It is at this point in the sleep cycle that we begin to really enjoy the profound healthful benefits of sleep. Our muscle relaxation becomes complete. Blood pressure drops and respiration slows. We are finally getting to total relaxation. While a tremendous benefit, stage three is only a precursor of the even greater sleep benefits to the fourth and deepest stage of sleep.

Stage four—Pure Delta slow wave sleep—yields profound and critical results for optimal functioning of body physiology and survival. <u>This stage is known for its healing and growth inducing properties.</u>

Blood supply to the muscles is increased in delta sleep. During this state the healing of every day muscular and micro soft tissue damage takes place. In fact, it is a current theory that patients who have been diagnosed with fibromyalgia have developed the disease because they do not get into the deeper fourth stage level of sleep. Interrupted sleeping patterns prevent or limit the healing benefits of sleep, by causing us to never experience the full cycle (stages 1, 2, 3, 4, and REM sleep) of sleep stages. You must experience all the stages of sleep to receive the benefits. In fact it is an all or none proposition. You either experience all stages of sleep and receive the benefits or you sleep in an interrupted pattern and receive virtually none!

Also, in the fourth level and deepest stage of sleep your body temperature reduces. This physiological body response <u>conserves energy</u>. Reduction of temperature also reduces metabolic activity, allowing more of your energy to be directed at repairing tissues. In younger children and teenagers this "redirection and conservation of energy" is vital for the individual to experience proper growth patterns. Growth hormone is secreted *only* when the pituitary gland reaches its twenty-four hour peak cycle. That occurs in deep sleep. Uninterrupted, sufficient sleep is so very important to a child's development.

As if this is not enough, there are farther reaching health benefits from deep sleep. Immune system "balance" is a hot topic today. Just observe the glut of remedies on the market claiming to give you an immune system boost. Without getting into specifics, the deeper levels of sleep greatly regulate your immune system, giving you increased resistance, particularly to viral infections.

When you are sick, when you are down, when you are depressed, *when you are tired,* you experience more flues, more colds, and more infections, due to a suppressed immune response. So, along with increasing your intake of fruits, vegetables and water intake, breathing better and getting your structure in tune, you are going to get enough deep sleep. It keeps that immune system active and alert. So start catching up on your sleep. It sure beats flu shots!

We're not done yet! In the deepest levels of sleep you experience a great many benefits related to "old age". You improve your ability to retain information. You improve your ability to learn.

During the deepest level of stage four sleep, brain cells that contain the neurotransmitters serotonin and norepinephrine are inactive. Neurotransmitters are chemicals that allow the nerves to transfer their electrical impulses along the integrated nerve highway efficiently, thus allowing the nerve impulses to reach their appropriate destination (i.e. muscle, cell, heart, etc). Decreasing the use of neurotransmitters during deep sleep allows the body time and energy to create more of these incredibly important nerve chemicals. Through this deep sleep activity the supply of neurotransmitters is replenished for the next day, when you are awake, active and in need of their vital presence.

These neurotransmitters are also crucial for learning and memory retention. By not sleeping and preventing the neurotransmitter supply from replenishing itself, you interfere with your ability to learn and remember. So before trying specialized brain supplements (or drugs) for your memory loss or for your lethargic brain function, why don't you try sleep? Also, sleep comes at an affordable price: it's free.

Sleep is critically important to optimum health and quality of life. It is a vital part of the Power Health Formula and is required to get your body, mind and spirit functioning optimally. The body *demands* eight to ten hours of sleep. Like it or not, <u>you cannot cheat nature</u>. You will never feel the well being available to you if you do not get an adequate amount of sleep. Do it!

Sleep Rules

1. Eight to ten hours. Few individuals can get by on five or six hours of sleep. If you are not following any components of the Power Health Formula, your optimum sleep requirement is probably ten hours. If you are following the Formula, you may be able to get away with seven and a half to eight hours. Very few people, even following the formula, can get away with six. So if you are "new on the path" please get eight to ten hours of sleep a night.

2. Go to bed at the same time every night, preferably before the 11 o'clock news. Go to bed at the same time every time *every* night (yes, including Fridays and Saturdays) **and** get up at the same time each morning. Do not try to catch up on lost sleep by sleeping in later in the morning. If you need to pick up extra sleep, go to bed <u>earlier</u> do not sleep later. Not "sleeping in" is a crucial point. Do not ignore it.

3. Wake up without an alarm clock. I know this means many you are going to be late in the initial stages of your sleep training. But as you become sensitive to your sleep patterns you will not need an alarm clock. I have not used an alarm clock in fifteen years. I have never been late to work due to oversleeping.

4. Regularity and duration are the keys to developing deep sleep patterns. It is important to be regular with your arising and retiring hour seven days a week. Sleep occurs in cycles, each one lasting about one and one-half hours. When beginning the road to "health recovery" you need to get through at least five cycles to

experience the minimum physiological effects and advantages discussed in this chapter. During this hour and a half sleep cycle, you will process through the four stages of sleep. Each stage has a purpose and some benefits. You need to accomplish this one and a half hour cycle a minimum of five to six times a night to get the maximum health benefits of sleep. Regularity helps achieve this goal.

5.   Uninterrupted sleep is always the best. I do not care if you have to unplug your phone, put on blinders or kick your spouse out of the bed. If you want to get the most benefit from your sack time, be sure it's uninterrupted. Arrange your life so that when you are finished with your day, you can put all of your attention away and concentrate solely on relaxing and going to sleep.

I have also found that having a day planner and prioritizing my *daily* activities has helped me enjoy regular sound sleep cycles. That's right, planning my day helps me sleep better. Here is how and why.

First, I write down all of the daily activities I want to accomplish. Then I number them from one to whatever. Next I simply start at the number one activity. I accomplish that and I go on to number two. As I get each activity done, I check it off. If I only get through five of the ten activities, I do not worry about it, I just add the unfinished five activities to the next day's list.

I have found that one of the biggest culprits of my interrupted sleep patterns is thinking about what I did not get done that day. My mind then keeps thinking about my unfinished tasks while trying to sleep because it does not want to "forget" what needs to be done the next day. Writing it down each and every day means I don't worry about remembering. My mind can relax and go to sleep! To sleep more peacefully, try this little trick. It will help you.

When you have lost sleep, make up for it as soon as possible. If you have only slept six hours the night before, try to go to bed an hour or two earlier the next night. This is called a sleep debt. And as with every other debt in life, you must repay it as soon as possible or suffer the consequences.

71

6. Exercise and meditate. We have talked about exercise and we will talk about meditation. Numerous studies show that people, who exercise regularly, sleep much better and reduce their sleep requirement to 7-8 hours. Same applies to meditation.

7. Stop or reduce smoking, reduce caffeine, avoid alcohol. Studies have shown that alcohol within two hours of sleeping interrupts the sleep patterns, as do caffeine and smoking. Try not to have any caffeine after 2 o'clock in the afternoon.

8. Don't watch exciting, emotionally responsive movies right before bed. These movies stimulate nerves that keep playing the emotional parts of the movie all night long, interrupting the 4 stages of sleep.

Go back through this chapter, watch the video, listen to the cassettes, and learn the value of sleep. It's really easy. Just relax, close your eyes and sleep your way to Power Health.

The Mind

The mind body connection is a subject that has been justifiably receiving a lot of attention since the early 1970's. The mind body connection, using the mind and spirit to heal the body, should be a cornerstone of anyone's health care program. The scientific, health care, and medical communities still approach the entire subject with great caution and in trepidation. Though the spirit mind body connection has been utilized in healing traditions for thousands of years, our society's penchant for using methods that we can touch, feel and smell such as drugs and surgery remains a barrier to its inclusion in our "standard" health procedures. Science itself is fearful to embrace the mind body connection in healing and health wholeheartedly for fear of losing its prestige with its materialistic hard data thirsty following. Society and science should allay their fears because the mind body connection is very scientific and it is very real.

The mind body connection has interested medical practitioners and scientists for most of the twentieth century. For the last 500 years scientists have utilized a reductionist model of healthcare. In other words, reducing and dividing your body for analysis into its simplest parts (i.e. atoms, cells, organs, molecules, etc.). It was thought that by reducing the body into its simplest elements and analyzing each part that we would find the answers to sickness and disease. This thinking remains prevalent in today's research oriented society in which it is hoped to find a new gene for every disease. Then by correcting the genes, we will ultimately cure all diseases. I can tell you for the most part that this is not going to happen. The body works as a whole. You cannot take parts and fix them out of context to the rest of the body. You cannot even consider healing the body without healing the mind. Freud was probably one of the first people to recognize this and it is for that fact more than anything that his name has remained a household word, unfortunately.

Upon the recognition of the mind as part of our healing mechanism, science ultimately developed the field of psychiatry. But, once again, the field of psychiatry was an attempt to reduce the mind to its simplest elements and to separate the mind from the body. This is further reductionist theory. Instead of joining the mind with the body, we now had people trying to heal our minds and other people trying to heal our bodies. I would say that from the amount of sickness and disease we suffer and the high rate of heart attacks, strokes and cancers, that this approach has not been successful. There is no such thing as a purely physical or mental disease. All ailments have components of both. It has been said there are no incurable diseases, only incurable people. Thus our 500 year scientific romance with the reductionist physical and mental models of a pill for every physical symptom and a psychiatrist for every emotional condition must end and be replaced with the more comprehensive thousands years old healing model that addresses the whole - mind, body and spirit. For this reason the Power Health Formula employs both the physical <u>and</u> the mental approaches for experiencing maximum health, and if you are ill while you are reading this, for helping you to approach any illnesses you might be attempting to heal at this point in time.

To this end, the mind's role in healing must be scientifically addressed in *any* text on healing or it cannot be considered a comprehensive text on the subject. In my opinion, a huge turning point in understanding the reality of the mind's healing power utilizing meditation, prayer, affirmation and visualization and why they work came from the basic research of Dr. Candace Pert, Ph. D.; a former chief of staff of the section of Brain Biochemistry of the Clinical Neural Science Branch at the National Institute of Mental

Health.   Dr Pert is the researching scientist who discovered endorphins. You have all heard of endorphins, but what are they and why were they such a monumental discovery?

Endorphins are neuropeptides. Neuropeptides are the body's internal pain relievers. More than that, neuropeptides are messengers. They are messengers that in addition to the integrated highways of the nervous system communicate signals from your brain to every single cell in your body.   Dr. Pert was able to show that located on the surfaces of our cell walls are receptor sites that receive these messenger molecules, message molecules that are triggered by thoughts from the brain. So every thought that we have is not only emanated and sensed in the brain but also is communicated physically throughout the body to each and every single cell.

Dr. Pert further demonstrated that depending on the emotion that your thoughts were expressing, specific actions would be taken by the cells accordingly.   In other words, your cells physiologically respond according to your positive or negative emotional output. Cells either function pro-actively to positive emotion, to be healthy and to perform their normal functions, or cells would actually shut down and protect themselves relative to the brain's negatively expressed thoughts. It was also demonstrated by Dr. Pert that these messenger molecules, strongly influenced by the emotion of the thought, are intimately related to the function of the all-important human immune system. The action of a thought communicating to a cell and creating a certain response appears to be the juncture at which point the body and the mind are no longer distinguishable from one another. The mechanism of messenger molecules from the brain communicating to the cell through receptor sites and influencing the physiological response of that cell is the scientific demonstration of the mind body connection. No longer can mind body concepts be considered only in the realm of metaphysics.

These advances in cellular science signify an evolutionary turning point. For at least the last fifty years we have held the belief system that our health and our fate were preprogrammed in our genes. The significance of this change in paradise is immense because the implications of understanding that our thoughts affect our cells physiology and behavior goes even further than the fact that positive mental attitude is not a joke. It implicates that our thoughts affect our cells internal metabolism and contents, which include DNA and RNA, our genetic materials.

A long held scientific belief is that the character of one's life is genetically predetermined. Cutting edge scientists, who are bucking the system, are promoting a radically new understanding of the unfolding of this leading edge of science indicating that our thoughts actually determine our genetic makeup. This could explain why spouses start to look like each other after so many years, why animals tend to resemble their masters or why an adopted child will begin to appear genetically related to their totally non-genetically related parent. Is it the continual observation and thought patterns resulting from these relationships that change the genetic characteristics and cause physical changes? It is beginning to appear that way.

Even cellular biologists are now acknowledging that the environment, your perception of the environment, and the thoughts that you create and communicate to your cells as a result of that perception of the environment directly controls not only your cellular activity but probably the activity of the very genes of your body as well.

The mind body connection had been discovered in India, China, Central and South America, Egypt and probably parts of Africa thousands and thousands of years ago. This concept of the body and its self healing capability has been severely criticized by modern medicine because of these ancient cultures did not have access to the "advanced" medical methods and equipment or the scientific research and methods that we have today. These ancient cultures did however spend *thousands* of years using awareness as their scientific instrument and the nervous system as their laboratory. Which once again just proves to me that as a complete whole human being, that *we are enough* and we are capable of knowing and understanding just about anything. It is difficult if not downright irrational to question the conclusions of thousands of years of clinical observations in the mind body field and to dismiss these findings as unscientific. With

Dr. Pert's work the mind body connection has now transcended modern medicine and scientific prejudice and snobbery and crossed over from the subjective use of awareness and understanding to the very modern laboratories of cutting edge maverick scientists who are proving that indeed *you are what you think.*

Meditation

I remember when a friend first tried to introduce meditation into my daily routine. I often wish that at the time I had not held the strong beliefs, prejudices and values systems that had been taught to me in my previous twenty-five years on this planet. I remember driving to the home in which the meditation classes were being taught. I was ushered into a room which displayed a great many mystical and eastern trappings. Incense was lit and I was sat down and given a long dissertation on meditation, its history and its effects. The religious implications that these well-meaning teachers were attempting to foster upon me were in direct conflict with my strict Roman Catholic upbringing and as a result created a wall of resistance to my accepting meditation as a valid discipline. It took me many years to understand that the wall of resistance was simply a misunderstanding of the true "technology" of meditation. Despite my intrepidation, I decided to give meditation a try anyway. So I endured the incense, I endured the incantations, I endured the eastern mysticism and mystery, which surrounded the darkened room with the lit candle and the fan blowing in its rhythmic vibrations, and I began my journey inward.

I was given a mantra and I was told that it was very sacred and that no one could ever know my mantra. I was given many, many specific instructions which really made it difficult for me to implement this system into my life. Though I tried for months, I was never able to sustain the discipline and I let it drop from my life for years.

But as my understanding of the mind body connection continued to expand, I decided that I had to comeback to the discipline of meditation and strip from it all the trimmings and trappings that really have nothing to do with actual act and discipline of meditation. I realized that I had to utilize some sort of introspection in my own life if I wanted to use the power of my mind and my spirit to help calm, focus and heal my own body.

Today, the art and science of meditation is becoming a part of mainstream health concepts. Time spent in meditation at the very least serves the purpose of stress reduction and physical healing. Some would say it is a time that you use to connect with your religious or philosophical core and to move your personal evolution forward, focusing on ideas of healing, service and spirit. It is not to the latter that we address this book although we do not deny that we believe that there are spiritual benefits to be had from years of practicing the discipline of meditation. It is this latter aspect of meditation, however, that initially I find wrongly turns a great many people off (as it did to me). The religious/philosophical facet of the practice is not an aspect of meditation that has to be utilized or addressed by the meditator to use it for health related purposes.

As a part of the Power Health Formula, we use meditation strictly as a technique for stress reduction, relaxation and for the positive physiologic effects that meditation has on the physical body. We have attempted to strip meditation of its religious and cultural trappings, sticking to the art and science to make it appropriate for you to use this very basic and simple and powerful method to your advantage, no matter what your religious or philosophical beliefs.

How do you meditate? Learning meditation is just like learning any other acquired skill. You learn to meditate just as you learned to walk. You begin at the beginning. First you crawl, then you try to get up on two legs. Then you fall down. You pick yourself up and you fall down again. Eventually you get to the part where you can walk. Walking ultimately begets running, and the process is complete. You have to accept the fact that as you learn to meditate you are going to experience good and bad meditating days. It is a process of learning. This is why I refer to meditation as a discipline and it will require a certain focus for you to persist and stay on the path. I suggest that before you undertake the act of meditation, you get very clear on your purpose for meditating, maybe even write that purpose down and have it in front of you first thing in the morning before you meditate.

My own purpose for meditating was very simple. At the time that I explored the discipline of meditation, I felt that the problem of my health was the most vital problem of my life. I felt that everything in my life depended upon my having ultimate health. Peace and happiness, my accomplishments in the different spheres of my life, my attitude, my behavior with others, the very significance of my existence all seemed to depend upon my health. I did not have good health or health habits at the time I started this journey. I was very ill. I had a very addictive, compulsive, obsessive, behavioral type of thinking. My mind was continually going at a million miles an hour. I felt that for me to break the compulsive, addictive type of thinking that had developed in my computer-like brain, I needed to use a method that would allow me to not only experience health benefits but get control of my mind and use it to my benefit in facing and making changes in my health habits. Habits that were vital for me to accomplish—my goals. This goal, this purpose, I wrote on a piece of paper and reviewed every morning before I sat down to meditate. As a matter of fact, I reviewed it before I went to bed at night so that it would give me enough initiative to get up in the morning and to be disciplined enough to perform my meditation. So I suggest you get very clear on why you want to meditate. Write it down. In fact why don't you take some time and do that right now.

Now that you have your purpose for meditating written down, here is how I do it. Upon arising, I have a glass or two of water. This seems to help hydrate my body and put my mind in a better physiological mode to meditate. I then walk around the house for a little bit or I might take a walk outside. But I give myself about ten or fifteen minutes to get my physiology moving. I might take the dog for a walk. Hopefully, in that period of time if I have to move my bowels or urinate I will do so, because these are urges you do not want to have occur in the middle of your meditation. You need to eliminate as many "bodily" distractions as possible. In this vein, I will do a few stretches to get my body slightly supple and prepared for sitting in one quiet spot for ten to thirty minutes.

For step number two, I sit down in a room and in the spot that I have chosen for meditation. I strongly suggest that you choose the same room and the same spot every day. The room should be quiet. It should not have a telephone in it or you should temporarily disconnect the telephone. The rest of the family should know that when the door to this room is closed, it means that you are not to be disturbed and that this is more or less a sacred time in your life. You are taking time for yourself, to be with yourself and that they should respect that. Once you have sat down into the chair (I suggest a chair, it is more comfortable than the famed lotus position. It is not necessary to use lotus position to get results) you should then read your purpose for meditating and get very clear on why you are taking this valuable time out of your life to sit down and to perform the discipline that we are going to talk about in the next few steps. This is a vitally important step. Do not skip it. Believe me, you are going to need it on those days when you feel like you are wasting valuable time or when you do not feel like meditating or the day after you had a not so great meditative experience.

The next step is for you to get ready. When I say that, I mean that you need to get your body in its most ready "relaxed" physical condition to meditate. This is not difficult. First of all, please, as stated above, you have found a decent chair in which you can sit in. Preferably a chair in which your feet will hit the ground comfortably and in which you can sit with your spine straight. As mentioned above, you do not need to master the lotus position. I remember when I was first introduced to meditation, it was by some folks who were disciples of the Hindu meditative techniques and they insisted that I needed to use the lotus position. Sitting cross-legged on the floor with my spine straight and with my head looking at a 45° angle upward. This was a very difficult position for me at the time due to the fact that I was very inflexible and it hurt my meditative experience because I spent more time being concerned about my posture and the pain that it was causing me, than trying to focus on the purpose of what I was trying to accomplish mentally and spiritually. Relax on the dogma. Use a chair, sit straight up, feet flat on the floor, hands preferably not folded but gently, comfortably lying on your lap, shoulders relaxed and head as straight as possible without straining.

The next step is to perform a breathing exercise. I suggest that you use the following Yoga breathing exercise that was taught to me by an Ayeradic health practitioner. It is very simple, it is very calming and it is very powerful. It consists of breathing in through the left nostril while holding your right nostril closed with the thumb of your right hand, then breathing out through your right nostril while releasing your thumb and holding your left nostril closed with the middle finger of the same hand. Repeat the breathing in through your left nostril and breathing out through your right nostril three times. Then switch. Breathe in through the right nostril and out through the left, using the same finger maneuvers, obviously in reverse, continuing to use the right hand. Do this three times. Then, remove your hand and breath in and out through both nostrils three times. If you are not in a hurry, and you should not be because the purpose of meditation is to break you from the habit of being in a hurry, I would suggest that you repeat this entire cycle three times. This will put you in a relaxed physiological breathing state (you are probably diaphragmatic and abdominally breathing by now) that will enable you to get the maximum benefit from your meditation.

The next step to successful meditation is further relaxation. Very simply go through all the "tight" parts of your body. Mentally relax them. Relax your feet, your calves, you upper legs, your buttocks, your abdomen, your upper back, your chest, your upper arms, and your forearms in this order. It is very important to then relax your hands, relax your neck and still as importantly, relax the muscles in your face. Do not get too uptight about this procedure. The relaxation "procedure" is about relaxing. Just let go of each muscle group and go on to the next. This preparation should only take about three minutes. You are now ready to meditate.

I prefer the simple ancient technique that was first discovered by the Buddha. I need to acknowledge the Buddha. This is his technique. For those who have a religious aversion to Buddhism (I am not a Buddhist or a Hindu) understand that at the time that the Buddha was the Buddha, he was not a Buddhist, he was simply a prince who had been sheltered from the world by his parents. One day, he went out from his sheltered palace and into the world. Seeing its pain and anguish for the first time, he wanted somehow to correct it. The thing I liked about the Buddha was this gentleman was into simplicity in its nth degree. As part of his quest for the answers to all questions, he came up with a simple meditative technique which is not spiritual, it is not religious and if anything, it would probably have to be called secular. The Buddha's technique is simply to focus on your breath as it travels in and out of your nostrils.

So back to meditation. You should now be relaxed. Begin to concentrate on your breath traveling in and out of your nostrils. Focus on your breath coming in your nostril…now focus then on your breath exiting your nostril. Do not attempt to control or change your breathing pattern. Just notice and observe your breathing. That is all. This is your entire goal for the next fifteen or twenty or thirty minutes, whatever time length you feel is maximally beneficial for you.

What you will experience is that mind of yours, that is going a thousand miles an hour, will resist your concentration on something so simple as breathing. So every time you get a thought that interrupts your pattern, you need to gently, easily, calmly (not angrily), gently bring your mind back to focusing on the breathe going in and going out of your nostrils. That's it. That's the technique in its entirety. Cool huh?

Meditation takes discipline, otherwise it is this simple. It is beyond the scope of this manual to discuss all the potential benefits and experiences that you will be receiving from practicing this simple procedure day in and day out for the rest of your life. When you can focus on your breathe totally for five, then ten, then fifteen, then twenty minutes you will gain profound mental and physical benefits beyond anything you would believe even if I tried to describe it to you now. And truly, the experience is different for everyone, as it should be.

I will however, just to encourage and entice you to get started, briefly go over some of the more accepted healing benefits of meditation.

Benefits of Meditation

There have been thousands of studies in the scientific literature published in the twentieth century verifying the positive physiological effects of meditation. Thanks to the sixties generation and their interest in alternatives to mainstream health care, most of those studies have been done since 1960 due to such luminaries as Harvard's Herbert Bensen. More and more studies in the field of meditation are performed every year. Bensen was the first researcher to play a central role in the discovery that meditation counteracted stress; thus reversing the body's fight or flight mechanism. It was also Bensen who first scientifically suggested that meditation decreases heart rate, decreases blood pressure, decreases oxygen consumption and respiratory rate and thus, creates a tremendous sense of relaxation. There has also been a huge influence from the transcendental meditation groups' driving research and studies in this field.

Studies conducted by a variety of research institutes have also shown that meditation is physiologically distinct from sleep. This is a point I feel needs to be clearly understood because a significant aspect of the Power Health Formula is sleep. Sleep is sleep—meditation is meditation. We have previously discussed specific aspects of sleep and the fact that we go through one and a half hour sleep cycles in which we hopefully reach a state called REM sleep. Remember there are several levels that we must travel through to get into REM sleep.

One of those levels is called alpha sleep. Alpha sleep produces alpha waves. Alpha waves are also abundant during meditation. In sleep clinics, however, alpha waves are rarely noted because it is such a fleeting part of the sleep cycle. But in meditation, these eight to twelve cycles per second alpha waves are abundant. In the alpha wave stage of meditation, your breathing rate slows dramatically, as do your brain waves. People have used biofeedback devices to try to train themselves to enter and sustain this relaxed alpha state in order to reduce high blood pressure, hypertension and headaches. You really do not need a biofeedback machine to achieve this state, just the simple meditative techniques that we have discussed in this chapter.

Though there are no studies to prove alpha states have major impacts on health conditions, it has been shown that the alpha wave state is relaxing and is something worth achieving in today's stressful society. So the meditative alpha state is distinct from the sleep alpha state in its duration and effects.

Also differing meditation from sleep is oxygen consumption. Oxygen consumption drops in sleep. But it drops at only a rate of about five to eight percent below your waking rate during the entire sleeping period of five or six hours. In meditation the oxygen consumption rate also drops, but more so, about fifteen to twenty percent in only minutes. It may be this rapid oxygen consumption rate drop that is responsible for experienced meditators claiming that fifteen to twenty minutes of meditation seems to be equal to eight hours of sleep. I certainly am in the camp that claims fifteen minutes of meditation feels like several hours of sleep because I experience it on a daily basis. I meditate for a second time daily at 1:30 in the afternoon before I see my 2 p.m. patients. After this brief meditation, I am completely and totally rejuvenated and alive again. And my energy levels are optimum. So do not think you can drop your meditation even though you are sleeping eight to ten hours. Sleep and meditation accomplish different mental and physiological benefits and are separate and distinct important aspects of the Power Health Formula.

The benefits of meditation probably would require a thousand page tome to chronicle completely. But there is one more aspect of meditation worth mentioning. I have noticed in my practice that meditation helps patients to reduce pain. It has been demonstrated in scores of studies that a variety of pain syndromes have responded to meditation in patients who have been unresponsive to medication and other standard medical treatments. Studies have also shown improvement in pain from muscle tension, headaches, low back pain, painful menstruation and a multitude of other entities. I have had the opportunity to observe this phenomenon of mind over matter frequently in over twenty years of treating all of the aforementioned conditions. So, meditate. Make it a part of your life. Make it a daily routine for the rest of your life. Spending quiet time with yourself is not an option if what you are after is true abundant Power Health.

For those of you who are still not able to disconnect the fact that meditation is not a religious or philosophical discipline and to feel that you have a need to connect with your religious and philosophical core, please feel free to use prayer to achieve the spiritual and physiological effects that the mind holds. In fact, let's discuss the health benefits of this age-old practice.

Prayer

I grew up in a weird relationship with prayer. Being raised in a strict, Roman Catholic family I was exposed to what I thought to be severe doctrine. My life was dictated by a variety of rules and restrictions, standards which seemed to me impossible to live up to. By the time I was twelve, I was absolutely certain that if there was a heaven and a hell, I was definitely going down in flames. It was certainly a depressing thought, especially at the age of twelve years old and with my whole life ahead of me. There were moments in which I wondered if it was even worth going on.

But I had a concept of spiritualism and God even at that early point in my life. That, in retrospect, surprises me even to this day. The one part of my religious dogma and indoctrination that made complete sense to me was prayer. Talking straight to whoever God was, whatever God was. It felt good. It was probably the only thing that prevented me from committing suicide. Prayer was my lifeline. I did not know what it was, I wasn't even quite sure who I was praying to. I certainly did not understand the physics or the mechanics of it nor did I care. All I knew was that it made me feel good. The more I prayed the better I felt. I certainly said my basic Lord's prayer and Hail Mary's as many times as anyone could ever need to. I have come to experience tremendous value by meditating on the positive thoughts presented in these prayers.

It was not very long before I started making up my own prayers. Prayers that had particular meaning to me. Prayers that got me through the moment, got me through the hour and got me through the day. The more I prayed, the more I really felt as though there was someone who was really listening, someone who really cared. In watching the every day occurrences of my life, I actually started to

85

believe that there was an entity who was answering my most heartfelt needs. I have never been able to shake the feeling (not in my entire life…) that prayer is very real, that someone or something is listening, and that someone or something seems to keep helping me along the way.

As life went on, I became a lot more "rational" and started to question the essence of prayer. I was always blessed with skill in the sciences; biology, chemistry, organic chemistry. I particularly loved physics. Einstien is my man! As my life started to take on a more rational, intellectual and analytical flavor, I let prayer go and started to be heavily influenced by the writings of such luminaries as Ayn Rand, who basically is an atheist. A brilliant female philosopher and writer, she eschewed the notion of prayer being of any value whatsoever. As the discipline of prayer began to leave my life, I started to get a little less comfortable and a lot more stressed. Suddenly it was as though there was no one to talk to. Certainly, I am a proponent of standing alone in life and being self-reliant. But it did not feel good.

I must tell you that my life lacked quite a bit of luster during those years in which I chose to ignore those little voices that were so instrumental in saving my life in my younger years. As I wandered farther and farther away from my spiritual center, my life became chaotic, stressful and almost unbearable. An interesting phenomenon I have experienced myself and observed in others is that once our life deteriorates to such a point that we cannot take it any more, it is at the point that we resort to prayer. And, certainly, that occurred with me. I hit bottom and started to pray.

As I said earlier, I am a student of physics with Einstein being probably my greatest mentor. As it turned out, it was Einstein who brought me back to a life of prayer. In his search for the unified field in his unified field theory, he was led indeed to whatever you would like to call it, but most people tend to call it God.

"The most important human endeavor is striving for morality in our actions. Our inner balance and even our very existence depend on it. Only morality in our actions can give beauty and dignity to life."

Albert Einstein

I am so grateful that in pursuing a career in physics, a career that I obviously never culminated, I was led back to the very essence of our existence and a method for contacting that deep, spiritual oneness inside of me that makes me complete and whole. I no longer believe that we must choose between the rational and the intuitive or the analytical and the spiritual or the intellectual and the emotional.

There is ample scientific evidence available today to demonstrate the healing power of prayer. For those who wish to use prayer, there is no question that prayer compliments, though in many cases may not take the place of, good health care habits, alternative care and/or medicine. It comforts me that prayer as well as meditation is compatible with modern physics and that if you asked a scientist today if he believes in God, a true scientist will say, "Of course I believe in God. I am a scientist."

Five hundred years ago, a scientist would have said, "Of course I do not believe in God. I am a scientist." The circle has been completed.

I have treated patients since 1979. I can tell you absolutely, 100% for sure, that a patient's beliefs and their doctor's beliefs in both their treatment and in the ability of that patient to get well, increases and in many cases determines the success of that patient's effort to heal. Those that used to be considered mavericks in the field of the mind body connection are now being justified by their clinical observations. Scientific data indicates that to have abundant health, or maximum healing responses, you must balance and harmonize the scientific and the spiritual, the material and the non-material. You do not have to understand the mechanics of mind body disciplines, all you have to do is experience the benefits of practicing meditation, prayer, and affirmation. It does not matter that you do not understand the physiological aspects of breathing or what occurs in your body as a result. All that is important is that you breath. Prayer follows the same law. If you genuinely pray you will get the benefits.

It is interesting that as I am writing this, I have received a phone call from my mother, who unfortunately is not very well. She is seventy-six years old and lives in Trenton, New Jersey. I live in Lake Tahoe, Nevada. We communicate regularly by phone. Our entire conversation this morning was based on the fact that under very difficult circumstances, the circumstances being the recent loss of my father, my mother's health is being heavily impacted by having to live alone for the first time in my mother's entire life. She is experiencing severe loneliness, which I believe has depressed her immune system, and thus Mom is now experiencing a variety of vague and non-definable illnesses which are making her sick and frightened. My mother finds her strength in prayer. My mother uses prayer, she uses holy water, she uses mass cards and she uses whatever she can in the form of prayer to give her strength every day. I continue to encourage her in these endeavors. In fact, there is not a day that goes by that I do not pray for my own mother's spiritual, physical and mental well-being. Indeed, she has indicated that it is only the process of prayer that helps her physical ills.

I pray for my mother confident that it helps her in some way. Prayer can be so powerful that even the receiver of the intention of a prayer can be powerfully benefited by it. In a random, double blind study, it was demonstrated that prayer had a statistically significant healing effect on hospitalized heart patients. The study was done at the University of California Medical School in San Francisco, California by a Dr. Randolph Byrd. This study included over four hundred patients who were divided into two different groups. Both groups were receiving medical care for their heart problems. However, one of the two groups was prayed for by members of Protestant or Catholic prayer groups. The patients, the doctors and the nurses did not know who was being prayed for. Half of the patients being prayed for did not know that they were being prayed for. The results rocked the medical community. Those heart patients who had been prayed for were significantly less likely to develop congestive heart failure and a full 80% required less or *no* antibiotics after the praying had been instituted. None of the patients in the group that were being prayed for required a mechanical ventilator or iron lungs. Twelve members of the group that was *not* being prayed for required this intervention. Those who were being prayed for contracted less of other types of diseases such as pneumonia. Fewer had cardiopulmonary arrests and during the period of the prayer trial, *none* of the patients being prayed for died, whereas three of the patients not being prayed for died.

Once again, prayer is an extensive topic, which probably requires volumes to thoroughly explore its mechanisms and benefits. It is not our intent to exhaust the topic of prayer in this brief instructive book. My intention is to supply you, the pursuer of Power Health, with the understanding that prayer is as real as the very paper and pen that I am using to write these words. (That's right, I do not use a computer!) You do not have to understand how prayer works, you just have to know that it does. If you come from a structured religious background that promotes prayer as part of its discipline, I suggest that you use it and experience the rewards.

How To Pray

It would be presumptuous of me to attempt to transcend or circumvent or add to the great traditions of prayer that have existed for thousands of years. Thus I will not attempt to do so. However I do believe that there are some basic praying "strategies" that can help each and every individual. Praying seems to be an urge that is with all of us. It appears to be unconscious, innate, instinctive and intuitive.

More often than not, your subconscious, spiritual self knows what you need to pray for on any particular given day and time. The best advice to you is follow your instincts. Even if they do not make any sense, follow your instincts. You may be feeling strong and praying for success. It is okay, pray for success, follow your instincts. You may be feeling weak and you may need to pray for courage and/or strength. If that is what your instincts tell you then that is what you should be praying for. You do not need to have a standard meditative prayer that you use each and every day, although at times in my life I have utilized prayers from different traditions that have, I believe, pointed my life in directions that I needed to take. For about one year of my life, having no background in Hindu tradition, I used a verse from the Bhagavad Gita. It was a favorite verse of Mahatma Ghandi, another one of my spiritual mentors. I have also used prayers from Saint Francis of Assisi and the Bible. Many of these prayers would almost be considered affirmations due to the fact these prayers communicated to the universe specific desires and reinforced in my mind qualities that I wanted to become real in my spiritual and physical being. Prayer is a very personal experience. It changes from day to day, week to week and from one period of life to another, depending on where you are in life. Follow your instincts. No one knows better than you.

The second step in praying, as in meditation, is to get silent and to be alone. There are several ways to do this. This may sound funny, but one of my favorite things to do, when I decide to pray, is to pray while I am running. I run for thirty to forty-five minutes several times a week. When I run, after a few minutes, I will get into a kind of quiet, silent, meditative state. Then I might repeat a structured prayer or I might pray on a matter that is particularly on my mind that day. A more common way to get silent is to pray in bed, at night after you have been quiet for a while. This is a quiet time when you can relax and focus. Praying before sleep allows you to decrease the stress in your life and get a better night's sleep. Certainly praying first thing in the morning, maybe even before you get out of bed while you are still peaceful and calm from your five cycles of sleep can sometimes, in fact most of the time, set the tone of the day and put you more in control of the way your day unfolds. So you want to be firmly in control of your environment at the time that you pray and thus, you should in a quiet space.

The last aspect of praying is position dogma. I do not believe that you need to genuflect and/or kneel to pray. Praying is a personal issue between you and whatever or whomever you believe the entity to be to whom you are praying. I pray laying down, I pray running, I pray sitting, I pray when it strikes me. The less conditions that you set for having to pray (or for that matter having to do anything, including eat, exercise, meditate and sleep), the easier it is going to be for you to follow through on these recommendations. So, please, do not make this into some huge, difficult, ceremonial procedure. Although I feel prayer is sacred, prayer is simply a matter of you communicating with that quiet, spiritual place inside of you the thoughts that are congruent and important with who you are and what you are experiencing that moment.

The next step of prayer is intention. You need to have a heartfelt emotional intention to pray. It is this heartfelt emotional intention that will indeed direct your prayers. It is this heartfelt emotional intention that will tell you what it is you will be praying to and/or for that day. Do not get intellectual about praying. There is an old saying and I do not remember who said it, but it says that, *"Words are not as important as thoughts. Thoughts are not as significant as feelings and feelings are not as valuable as beingness."* You want to pray from your beingness and emotions as these are the deepest aspects of you, your thoughts and your needs. You need to listen to that voice inside and realize what it is you are praying for and then follow that. The success of prayer has everything in the world to do with your intention. If you are praying sincerely, and if what you are praying for is congruent with who you are and what you are feeling, your belief system in that prayer will be unshakeable. If you have an unshakeable prayer belief system, it will affect communication of your thoughts to whoever and whatever entity you are communicating. Hearfelt, genuine, sincere prayer will create miracles. Always remember, your intention of prayer needs to be unshakeable and certain. The way to accomplish this end is by praying on that which comes from your heart.

Lastly, do not make this complicated. Just pray. Nature will take care of the rest. Pray what's in your heart and soul and you may learn what it is to experience the power of daily miracles in your life.

91

Affirmations and Visualizations

In my life, affirmations and visualizations go together, thus we will cover them as such because that is how I utilize them. I was first exposed to both of these procedures when I was in college. I played two varsity intercollegiate sports. Mental discipline was required to help me prepare for each event. It was 1970 and motivational speakers were exploding onto the scene at the time, and sport psychology was in its infancy. There were now famous studies involving basketball players practicing visualization in foul-shooting techniques versus basketball players who were actually performing the physical practice of shooting foul shots. The results were that the visualization group improved just as much as the group that was performing the physical task of foul shooting. Thus, in the early seventies, visualization and affirmation became a part of the sport psychology scene.

As I became exposed to these disciplines, I realized that I had been using them all my life. In the areas of my life in which I had already been successful, it apparently had something to do with my using both techniques. As a young baseball player in Little League, I can remember regularly going to bed in the evening, lying there and some would call it daydreaming—but I would say visualizing myself winning the game. Getting the winning hit, hitting the winning single or homerun, making the winning pitch and continuing to reinforce the fact that I was enough and able to make the play. In later years, in my endeavors to be a better golfer and with my limited ability to spend hours and hours and hours on the practice green, I decided to sit at home and visualize my swings, my putts and actually play mental rounds of golf on the golf course. As I would do this, I realized that my mental visualizations were actually affecting my nervous system and I could feel, as I would take a visual swing, whether the ball was going to go to the right or go to the left or straight down the middle. I could feel different muscle groups and how they were working. I was able to make physical corrections in my golf swing according to my visual images. This was all very basic to me and very real. Visualization was a method that I continued to employ throughout my entire sports career.

Affirmations were almost a way of life for me although I never knew I was affirming anything. I must thank my father for being the first one to help me in using affirmations, even though that is not what he called them. I am basically short for a baseball player. I am just a shade under five feet seven inches. As a shortstop, this was considered a deficiency when being scouted by the major league scouts. As long as I can remember, I was always the smallest, tiniest, child in the class, the smallest ballplayer on the field and the smallest person in the room. My father, realizing that this could be a block, immediately started to have me affirm the fact that small is good, that small meant compact, that small meant powerful, that small meant I could fit into seats better on the bus. He continued to affirm throughout my whole life that small was good. It became so much a part of me that no one could ever make me feel insecure by calling me diminutive or a shrimp or whatever derogatory comment that they would conjure up in attempts to undermine my confidence.

It took a few years for me to actually feel the confidence that was brought to me by these very simple affirmations of my younger years. But I started to realize that I needed to use these affirmations in sports. Playing baseball, when I would get in a slump and was unable to hit the ball properly or when I would lose my timing, I would simply go home and affirm that I was a good hitter. I had always been a good hitter. I will always BE a good hitter. When I would walk up to the plate, I would affirm that very simple affirmation of *just hit the ball!* Instead of thinking of the negative, not striking out, I would think of the positive, hitting the ball. The more I focused on the positive of just hitting the ball, the more my physical mechanics obeyed the positive affirmation and simply fell in line. It saved me umpteen hours of taking batting lessons and worry about my right leg or left shoulder or my head or my timing. I learned that I simply could affirm and that my physical performance would follow.

I started to learn more sophisticated affirmations after graduation from chiropractic college. It was at the time I ventured into business and had to begin treating real patients. It was "put up or shut up time". No more academic BS. The results counted now. In my early years of practice, there were a great many moments of doubt. It is so true when they say, "Doctors are only practicing." When I graduated chiropractic college, I think I knew just barely enough to be dangerous. Many times I suffered a lack of confidence attack when my inexperience resulted in my not understanding a person's physical condition. Not only was I not yet skilled in treatment techniques but my lack of experience in understanding people or how to use basic communication skills to help people get through their problems were taking their toll on what little confidence I had left. I wondered how to change this situation.

I started using visualizations and affirmations again. I began visualizing my office full of people and I started seeing the type of people that I wanted to come in. I started seeing the numbers of people I wanted to come in. I started seeing people getting well. I affirmed that I was a good doctor. I affirmed that I was learning what I needed to, that I was doing a good job, that I would help these patients because the universe was providing me with cases that were just right for my skill level. I would wake up every morning and have to affirm, just to gain enough courage to get myself through the barrier of going to work and facing those first few patients of the day. It all seemed so natural to me even though I did not realize what I was doing.

I think affirmations can be most valuable when people do not begin with a spiritual base of any kind and may not be amenable to prayer.

Affirmations are a very mechanical and an effective method of telling the universe visually and subconsciously what you want.

Why affirmations? It is really not that complex when you understand the basics of how you and I develop as human beings. Most of us are born into a loving, caring family. This family usually has traditions that it adheres to. Those may be religious dogmas, they may be philosophical, they may be from traditional lineage based on their nationality. These cultural ideas, concepts and beliefs are genuinely and sincerely transferred to you, the child, in order to bring you into the environment of the family, an environment in which it would appear to be most appropriate for your life to unfold according to the parents who are raising you as a child.

As you continue to grow, you are exposed to a variety of belief patterns and systems that you take on as real. For the first seven to fifteen years of your life you are developing your personality and who you are. During this time, we generally accept most of the aforementioned belief patterns without questioning them. The belief patterns may come from well meaning clergymen, who have their specific religious beliefs or they may well come from teachers who have their specific social beliefs and value systems.

We are exposed to an avalanche of information designed to influence us each day. This comes in the form of the television, radio, newspaper, Internet, etc. All of these sources of information "with an agenda" are transferring to us, via imprints on our computerized brains, the belief systems and patterns of the information's originator. Some of it is overt while some is subliminal. Very little of it is in our best interest. God knows, we are overwhelmed with information today and unfortunately, most of it misinformation.

Both information and misinformation are received by our brains and accepted by our subconscious minds. The subconscious mind does not know real from unreal or true from false. It just records the information. It becomes part of who we are. What we decide to accept and/or reject is how we formulate our personalities and our very beings. It is for this reason you will hear me frequently refer to the belief patterns you are experiencing and the fact that these belief patterns are so vital to your existence. We allude to these belief patterns not only in the videotape presentation of the Power Health Formula but heavily in our affirmation tapes. I strongly suggest you purchase these products and use them to break any negative belief patterns that you would like to eliminate from your life.

And therein lies the problem. Much of the world's collective consciousness is negative. Most of the information you are exposed to on an hourly basis (the news) is negative. People are walking around in a conditioned state of fear and doubt that has been conferred to them by the powers that be. Many societal groups and agencies find it to their advantage to have us, as individuals, experience fear and doubt in our thoughts and decision-making capacities. It makes us more susceptible to accepting their agendas, whatever they may be. Certainly the government wants us to experience fear and doubt so that we do not question the aspect of supporting their bills and paying their taxes. Marketers for products in all industries need us to feel insecure and self-conscious so that we feel we need to buy their products to make our life better. Fear, uncertainty and doubt are well understood and widely used to control us.

The number of people and organizations wishing to control your programming is endless. Religious institutions want us in a constant state of fear and doubt. It is to their advantage that we believe that without their help we are not going to find our way to heaven or where ever it is that we want to go after our bodily lives have been extinguished. The newspapers are merchants of chaos and mongers of fear, wanting to keep us on the edge so we buy their product day after day. To find out what is supposedly going to happen next in our lives, we listen to the newscasters on radio and television. They produce the source of fear and doubt, then make us feel that by listening to them daily we can allay our fears by programming us to believe that if we are up on the latest news we can avert the latest disaster. Most everyone that I know is insecure to some degree and for some reason. To try to get ahead in life each of us intentionally or unintentionally exploits one another's insecurities in an effort to be secure ourselves. This is so essential for you to understand. This is not an opinion and not a theory. This is the way that it is.

What ultimately happens is that we become negatively programmed. We wake up in the morning and think the world is terrible. This is going to be a difficult day. This is a bad situation. Challenges are no good. Change is no good. Problems are no good. Living is no good. Dying is no good. By the time we get to the age of twenty, we are so overwhelmed with negativity that it really becomes a challenge to get through the day. You must understand and accept this fact before you can wholly embrace the true value of visualization and affirmation. You must break this negative conditioning to be mentally and spiritually happy and physically healthy.

By simply observing the universe you can determine for yourself that abundant negativity in life is not the way that it was meant to be. If you take a long-term look at civilization, despite all the negativity, the evolution of mankind has been pretty much headed in an upward, positive pattern. There are some people who would disagree with that. But I am not one of them. Man has advanced rapidly over the last one hundred years because the limitations of the previous several thousand years have started to fall by the wayside. Man is becoming freer. If you observe the natural evolution of man you will see that it shows expansion. Man naturally wants to expand. Most people are always looking to improve themselves, to do more, to be more, to learn more. This is your natural instinct.

As I am writing this I am fortunate enough to be overlooking a forest. As I observe the forest, I see trees that are continually growing and have been growing for hundreds of years. I can observe the cycles of nature in which a flower that is outside of my window is pushing upward from underneath the ground to the side of the rock and then above the rock, even though the rock appears to be blocking its way. This is nature instinctively growing and expanding above, around and through its challenges. Man does the same.

The universe is expanding. Expansion by the way—is positive—not negative. We know that the natural fate of the universe is expansion. Observation of this fact over millions of years has led to the Big Bang

Theory because modern scientific techniques have been able to document the fact that the entire universe is expanding. Expansion is our natural state. Expansion goes along with improvement.

I believe that the world is not a bad place. Certainly it is challenging. I think that the restrictions and the challenges that we are faced with on this planet are part of life here on Earth. This is how we mentally, spiritually and physically grow or if you will - expand. To the degree that every one of you has faced one of these restrictions or challenges and has defeated it, you must admit you have felt better. You have mentally, spiritually and/or physically improved. You have probably also derived satisfaction from it.

So what has all this to do with affirmations? Affirmations and visualization are the tools to reprogram your computer from the negative input that overwhelms you each and every day of your life, and change that input to be positive, beneficial and healthful. For years, positive mental attitude gurus have been selling their wares on the market and there has been a great amount of criticism directed towards these people. I have had my own friends tell me that you cannot change who you are and you *should not* change who you are. They have told me it is impossible to change who you are. Well, I am here to tell you that *you can change who you are!* In fact, if you want change in your life the only thing *you can really change is you.* And better you be in charge of who you are and where you are going than everyone and everything else.

The way to change who you are is by reprogramming your computer to the positive and the beautiful. As you put positive thoughts into your mind, those thoughts are actually communicated to your cells, and to every structure in your body affected by those neuropeptides that we mentioned in our earlier discussion of the mind body connection. You not only can change your thoughts, which will change your physiology, but it is acknowledged now that it is very probable that you can change your actual genetic determination. Thus you can use your thoughts for any purpose you wish: feeling better, feeling less stressed, healing, material success, or improving future generations.

So how do you reprogram the computer? With affirmations and visualization. By affirming every day what you want out of life and by replacing the negativity that has been programmed into the "hardware" in your computer brain, you begin to look at life differently. You begin to see positive things in life, you begin to see beauty in life. You begin to see that you are not a bad person and that you were meant to be successful, that life was not meant to be hell on earth. It takes a little bit of work and it takes some consistency. But the results are worth the effort.

Understand that what we have discussed in this section is factual. This is *not* a theory. When you begin to change your thoughts, you begin to change your life, because your life is totally controlled by you. Scary, huh? Look around you. Whatever is around you, what you see and are experiencing is what *you and only you*, have created. You have created this life and environment by making decisions and following through or not following through with actions based on your beliefs and/or values. If you have yucky values, you are probably going to look around you and see that things are pretty yucky. If you are surrounded with beauty and positive things, good people and good friends, you have probably already been doing a great deal of the Power Health Formula including affirmations, prayers and visualizations. Your values, ethics and integrity are probably pretty solid. Your life circumstances are not an accident or an act of fate. You created them.

As mentioned previously, exercise is so crucial to the Power Health Formula that we devoted an entire video tape to a twenty minute exercise program that we feel is doable and will give you maximum results in a minimum period of time. With the same goal in mind, we have produced an audiocassette tape, which has my favorite positive thoughts and sayings and original music. The cassette is designed to empower you and to engage your emotions while you are listening to its affirmations and quotations. Music provides emotional input and helps drive these sayings, positive thoughts and affirmations deep into your subconscious to more effectively and more easily reprogram your mind. Remember Dr. Pert's work, emotion is the key in connecting your mind and your body. Emotion is where the mind and body meet. The music and the quotes engage your emotion and make the process fun.

Affirmations and visualizations simply reprogram your computer, better known as your brain, with information that honors you, empowers you, and allows you to take back control of your life.

How do you affirm? Again I remain true to simplicity in my methods of affirmation and visualization. You should too. There are a variety of methods for affirming. I will describe the one I use. But, first a few more words about affirmations.

Many millions of thoughts are programmed into your subconscious at this point in your life. You cannot change them all and you do not have to. All you have to do is change the key thoughts. How do you know what your key thoughts are? Listen to that little voice inside that told you what to pray for. The voice knows. Whatever challenges are facing you that day, are usually the challenges that you need to deal with. Thus, if you are dealing with difficulties in putting the program into place, you may need to listen to and/or create affirmations that are key to change, discipline, persistence or determination. You can use affirmations for absolutely anything that comes up in your mind.

What is the key to affirming? You must first believe that it works; we are affirming not wishing. You must know your mental affirmation will manifest in the physical universe. It must be a positive affirmation and it must contain emotion. It must be about something that really means something to you. You must also make the affirmation in the present tense. Your subconscious mind doesn't know the past from the future. It only knows the present. If you want to be disciplined, use the words, "I am disciplined. Discipline gives me freedom and independence. I do my daily exercise and use food as a high-octane fuel. Discipline sets me free." These affirmations exemplify using affirmation for discipline in the present and positive tense.

Again, always make the affirmation positive. Do not make it a negative. Do not say, "I need to get better at discipline." That is not a positive, strong thought. It indicates to the universe that you have a need and having a need is, in essence, negative. It is saying you do not have it, you are not enough and you want the universe to provide it to you. You always want to make a very positive statement - "I am disciplined and my freedom is expanding." "I never get lazy."—is not a great affirmation. "I am strong, energetic and disciplined."— would be a positive affirmation and would be much more effective than using "I never get lazy". Affirmations need to be positive.

Though I am going to share with you some of my affirmations for each area of the Power Health Formula at the end of this chapter, affirmations are most valuable if they come from you. Whether you are trying to deal with aspects of instituting a good diet, learning to pray, meditate, exercise or whatever, you have certain feelings, beliefs and values that have already been programmed into your computer over the period of your lifetime. Only you know what that programming is.

We have learned that strong belief and emotion is the key that links the mind and body. Only you know what emotionally moves you. Only you know what words will emotionally make you do what you need to do. Thus, you can use our affirmations as a starting point to get "the hang" of what the act of affirmation entails. Ultimately, if other words pop into your mind that mean more, that give you more emotion, these affirmations are going to be more valuable in achieving your goals. Go with those phrases. By all means, try not to intellectualize this information when it comes from your intuition because it is usually your intuition accessing parts of your subconscious computer, telling it that it needs to give to you because you are focusing on certain areas of your life. Always use your intuition, go inside and do it.

I review my affirmations immediately after my meditation. Why? Because, at this time, I am in a very clear space. My mind is focused, clear and calm. The words seem to get driven into my subconscious more effectively during this period of time. I spend approximately five minutes at the end of my meditation thinking about the type of person I want to be and the things that I want to accomplish that day and reciting the affirmations that I need to create my life as I wish it to be.

Visual affirmations can also be used. I have a bulletin board in my office. Whenever I intuit a goal I want to achieve, I either procure a picture of that goal, if it is something material, or I will write an affirmation relative to the goal and post it on the bulletin board. It then becomes as visual reminder to me and is something I can observe many times during the day.

Remember, you are reprogramming your computer for happiness, health and success. Your computer is processing thousands of thoughts per hour, most of them negative. Don't believe it? Then try—for *one* minute - not to think a negative thought. Do it now. Minute up? Couldn't do it, could you! Probably didn't last 15 seconds. You need to change that. You must combat those negative thoughts all day long. It's a challenge—and it's difficult but stick with it. As you program yourself using affirmation, you will find that eventually you will receive a negative thought. Use a positive affirmation to push those negative thoughts out of the way and replace them with the affirmation thought form. That is how affirmations work.

So what about visualization? For visualization, I follow the same method that I follow for meditation except at the end of my meditation and after my affirmations, I visualize whatever it is that I want in my life that day. I may visualize a meeting going well or treatment with a patient going well. If I am anticipating conflict, I visualize the conflict and envision myself resolving it to everyone's best interests. As I am visualizing a successful outcome, solutions come to me for the desired result. I believe in goal setting and I use visualization to set my goals. I visualize my patients getting well that day, how many patients I want to see, how many books I want to sell. I visualize my relationships and how I want them to be. I visualize every aspect of my life that comes to mind that morning because that is the visualization I need for that particular day.

Remember, you create your life. Until you understand and deeply believe the fact that you alone create your life and no one else is responsible for anything that has ever happened to you, you may have a difficult time getting motivated enough to visualize and affirm. You must get past the feeling that you cannot change or control events. Repetition of the processes of affirming and visualization are the key. If you don't believe, fake it until you make it become part of your thoughts, beliefs, value systems, decisions and actions. If you do not own this concept in your very soul, your affirmations will not work or will be weak. Understand this principle. You can change any aspect of your life that you so desire because you created it in the first place.

To further make visualization effective, it is best once you become more skilled at visualizing, bringing all six senses into a visualization. To do this, sit with your eyes closed but tilt your eyes up at a 45° angle because this engages your visual field. As you do that, visual pictures will more clearly enter your mind relative to the thoughts you are visualizing. Next I want you to sensually experience every aspect of what you are visualizing. If you are visualizing yourself abundantly healthy, you will *feel* yourself thin, you will *feel* your energy rise, you will *feel* what it means to be energetic. If you are visualizing yourself playing tennis, you also want to *smell,* the *smells* of the indoor or the outdoor court. You may wish to feel what it feels like to move your body around the tennis court. The more you can incorporate each one of your senses into your visualizations, the more clearly and definitely you will communicate to the universe exactly what you want and the universe will then be more likely to respond.

Remember this: the universe does not care. The universe does not care whether you win or whether you lose, whether you are fat or whether you are skinny, whether you are in great shape or whether you are in lousy shape. It seems to me the universe will give you exactly what you ask from it. Ask for negativity, you get it. Ask for success, you get it. The more input and the more clear you are in communicating to the universe, the more quickly and effectively your affirmations and visualizations will create your universe.

So communicate _very_ clearly and _very_ positively to the universe. When you master this component of the mind aspect of the Power Health Formula, you are going to start being very, very careful, not only about what you affirm and visualize, but about what you think during the day. What you focus on ends up being what you experience. What you focus on had better be what you want because I am going to guarantee you are going to get it.

The following are a few basic affirmations addressing various issues in your life. Use them to get started, play with them, fine tune them to meet your specific needs, change the words to words that will give you more of an emotional input, and make them yours.

Affirmations for Health and Healing

Every day in every way, I get healthier and healthier.

I am health.

My energy is unlimited.

My disease is a challenge and I am learning what I need to do.

I am firmly in control. I am strong, healthy, vibrant and energetic.

I stay well and I live well.

Affirmations of Positive Thoughts for the Mind

I am in control and I am ready to roll.

Calm and confident, I command my life.

I love my life.

I am what I am. I accept that.

I get what I focus on.

I am an unlimited being. My potential is limitless.

I am abundant. Abundance finds me.

Life is for living. I am living it to the max.

I am eating for life.

Sleep rejuvenates me.

I embrace sleep.

Exercise, food, sleep, balance.

Sleep focuses me. My efficiency soars.

I am handling my stress.

I am exercising my stress away.

I am important.

I honor myself.

Simple is powerful.

I trust my intuition.

Intuit, do it.

I am the Power.

Discipline

I am disciplined.

Discipline sets me free.

I set priorities and focus on one thing at a time.

I am starting today. I do it now.

There is no tomorrow.

In the famous words of Yoda, from "Star Wars", "There is no *try,* Luke, there is only *do!*"

Power

I stand up and claim my Power.

I express my Power and let it flow.

I am Power.

I use Power for the good of all.

What others think of me is none of my business. I only invest energy in things that resonate for me.

Miscellaneous affirmations that you can adapt for your own needs:

I am different and I am loving it.

I am different and I stand alone.

Abundant health is a habit with me.

I am lovable and I am loving myself.

I am working my doctor right out of a job.

I am enough.

Life is good.

I see only the beauty and the positive in all things.

Use these affirmations and the affirmations on cassette tape number two in the Power Health Formula Program to get started. See order form in the back of the book.

Once you experience the change that occurs in your life by focusing on the positive, by affirming and visualizing what <u>you</u> want out of life, you will never go back. A thousand years from now, all of mankind will be using their minds to produce the type of relationships, jobs, health, successes and abundance that they desire. Here is your chance to get a thousand-year jump on the rest of civilization. Use these affirmations and have fun. Good luck!

The Gradients of Health

Before we discuss implementing the Power Health Formula, there are a few more principles related to achieving and maintaining health that I would like to share with you.

The genesis of this entire program was my desire to break health habits and principles down to their simplest, most basic, most understandable elements. The Power Health Formula framework contains all you need to know to experience abundant health and success.

Unfortunately, in today's expanding information and technology society, most of us are dazzled and impressed by the complexity and sophistication of technology. Technology does have its place. But we are led to believe that the more complex and sophisticated our lives, the more advanced we become as human beings. I can assure you, nothing can be further from the truth.

While lecturing to thousands of people over the past ten years, there have been more than a few instances when I have debated the subject of simplicity versus complexity with audience members. I tell the proponents of complexity and sophistication that I have broken down the elements of each task I perform into its simplest and most basic components. This includes my work, my methods of treatment and my own health program. This approach has proven to be an extremely powerful and successful way to live. It has allowed me to remain focused, unconfused and effective in all areas of life. Life really is simple if we let it be.

Thus, one of the principles that you need to embrace, if you are going to experience abundance in life and the optimum health that I am sure you are seeking, is that *simple is powerful!*

The simple, basic design of The Power Health Formula is aligned with the laws of nature. I would seriously doubt that even a research scientist would ever find one aspect of this Formula that is lacking in its congruence with the natural evolution of the universe and, thus, the natural evolution and existence of mankind. Mankind is a part of nature's evolution.

Unfortunately, man is an egocentric being. Through incorrect training, disinformation and misinformation, man has come to see himself as being apart from nature rather than being a part of its evolution. This has been a detriment to most of mankind's quest for understanding, even for understanding the simplest principles of life and health.

Our minds, bodies and spirits must obey the same basic, simple laws of nature that are obeyed by not only the animal and plant kingdom, but by the very movement of the planets, moons and stars of the universe. When we align ourselves with these greater laws of the universe, we tap into its power. In doing so, we find less conflict in our life and less stress.

What we want, what we seek and focus on, comes to us much more quickly and in greater abundance. It is a principle simple enough for most to embrace. It is one to be aware of and accept. My understanding and acceptance of this law has resulted in success, happiness, health and the Power Health Formula.

Yes, the Power Health Formula *is* the law.

A law is a statement of what *always* occurs under the same conditions. For example: the law of gravity. The law of gravity is always consistent. It is invariable. You experience the law of gravity on Earth, you experience it in outer space, you are going to experience it on other planets, but you will always experience the law of gravity because it never changes. It always occurs under the same conditions.

The Power Health Formula will never change. This is why it is all you will ever need. If you wish to remove the confusion from your life, ignore today's fad and follow the Formula. The Power Health Formula is a distillation of the very essence of valid health disciplines and principles developed through the ages. It is a basic, powerful, simple to use, easy to understand Formula that, if followed, will be all you ever need to experience the feeling and abundance of the life you desire.

I am frequently asked, "Why does one particular vitamin, exercise, affirmation, medicine or surgery work for one person when it does not work for the next person?" My answer is that there will *never* be *one solution* that will work for every single individual. All of these "solutions" are offered out of context. Each "solution" addresses only one aspect of the Formula. The Power Health Formula works because it is a comprehensive, *integrated* approach to health excellence. It's the whole person that needs attention, not just one problem or symptom.

Most people accept the fact that every individual is different. People come from different genetic lines developed in different parts of the world. We have different emotions, thoughts, desires and attitudes. That is why we are called individuals. It would make sense that someone who comes from an Alaskan genetic line in the great far north would have different physical, emotional and spiritual needs and experiences than someone whose genetic line emanated from the equatorial regions in Africa and South America.

What is less obvious is that each of us is operating on a different gradient level of health. Let me explain. The word gradient is a derivative of the word graduation. Graduation is the concept of changing in steps or stages. For example, there are many gradations or financial stages between wealth and poverty. The same holds true for health. Depending on how many of the components of the Power

Health Formula you are presently incorporating (or more likely *not* incorporating), in your daily routine you will fall on a "health condition stage" somewhere between optimum health and death. There are more stages or degrees and gradations of health than there are colors in the rainbow. This critical concept explains why no two people can be treated exactly the same, whether with alternative or allopathic health care methods. Though your "gradient stage" may dictate which methods you choose to begin dealing with your health, eventually you will need to integrate all aspects of the Formula in your life to move up the scale.

At the bottom of the health gradient heroic and allopathic interventions are frequently appropriate. As you move up the gradient of health, alternative natural methods become more appropriate. The Power Health Formula defines the potential top of the gradient, the state of optimum health.

If you are following the Power Health Formula, you are ingesting the proper fuels, eating as cleanly as you possibly can. You are breathing well. You are drinking plenty of water and you are getting enough light. Your nervous system functions maximally, your blood and lymph fluids are flowing. Indeed, all of the fluids of your body flowing. You are exercising, in good shape and flexible. Thus your physical body is able to work the way it is supposed to while countering the effects of gravity. You are sleeping well, probably getting a minimum of eight hours of sleep each night, including 80% sound, uninterrupted sleep. Thus, you are going through all of the sleep cycles and getting all the benefits of regulating your immune, digestive, and cardiovascular systems. You are rejuvenating your mind and your ability to retain information and to think.

If you are working at the optimum gradient of health, you are meditating or using prayer, affirmation or visualization to get to that very peaceful, alpha state of being, where you relax and remove the pressure and energy demands from the body's system. This allows for relaxation, healing and repair. You are getting in touch with that spiritual being that is you and experiencing the positive effects of the universe.

111

A body is designed to work within the natural law and the universal confines of nature. When you are working within and with those laws instead of against them, you are experiencing more efficiency and more energy. You are experiencing less resistance and less stress. Your entire body is functioning maximally.

When functioning at maximum efficiency, your body's regulating mechanisms are better able to handle outside invaders, such as viruses and bacteria. When your body is working maximally you don't have to worry about pesticides in food or hormones in meat. With your body working efficiently enough you have the ability to process, cleanse and detoxify these elements right out of your system. Having an efficiently working body removes the need to accept the fears the media dishes out to you on a daily basis. Spiritual, mental and physical well being is your reward for incorporating the Power Health Formula. It puts you at the top of the gradient for optimum health.

At the other extreme of the gradient of health is the person who has done nothing in their life to allow their body to function optimally. This person never eats a vegetable. They eat erratically and when they do eat, they eat more food than their bodies can process. The foods that they eat cannot be processed properly and either turns to fat or negatively affects systems of their bodies.

They probably smoke, drink too much alcohol and are subject to the mindset that drugs are a solution to their problems. They are ingesting drugs on a daily basis, further putting poor fuels into their bodies. They probably never drink a glass of water, let alone eight glasses of a day and their fluid intake includes mostly caffeine-related products and carbonated beverages. They are more than likely chest breathers, creating not only a lack of oxygen to the system, but frequently a feeling of anxiety and a great deal of stress.

These folks are highly stressed out people who remain indoors all day at work, go home to sit in front of the television, sleep in their house, get up and do it again and again and again.

Because many of the people at the bottom of the health gradient never experience the light of day, their immune systems are shot. They are always tired. How are they going to have a good integrated highway? They are not, because they rarely get up and move.

Movement is life. Movement means walking. Movement means exercise. This person, at the bottom of the health care gradient, is the one that bought the concept that life should be easy, that all of the entertainment in the world is for them and they are experiencing a great life. They sit in front of the television for six hours a day, go to the movies, and do all of the things that society has told them is part of the good life. But there is virtually no movement in their bodies. There is no fluid movement, improper blood circulation, constriction of their joints and ultimately diseases like arthritis, low back problems, headaches, flues and colds. These people consider themselves sick, and for good reason. They are.

Is this person going to sleep? Probably not. The person at the bottom of the health gradient more than likely thinks that sleep is a waste of time, a terrible substitute for watching a late night talk show. Sleep is a practice they wish they could avoid. And avoid it they do. These folks tend stay out late, get up early and are stressed out because their jobs demand so much of them. In most cases their eating, drinking and smoking habits combined with lack of exercise negatively affects their ability to sleep anyway. They are probably one of the estimated one hundred million sleep deprived people in the United States.

You cannot have a functioning immune system or muscle tissue repair system if you are not getting your sleep. This causes further breakdown of the body. Certainly these are the folks that never take time for themselves. They do not use the mind to create optimum cellular function. They are negative in thought, deed and action. They do not even realize that they can reprogram their mind, usually rejecting the concept as stupid. Their reality says that life is yucky. Life happens. I have no control over it—it is negative, terrible and hell on earth. And the mind body connection communicates this to all their cells.

In my practice, I have seen people at the top of the health gradient pray themselves well. Unfortunately, more often, I have seen patients at the bottom of the health gradient affirm themselves sick.

113

Meditation, prayer, affirmation and visualization are not even in this person's reality structure and it certainly shows. What is the picture of the person at the bottom of the health gradient?

They are anxious and stressed. Why not? By the time this person has reached midlife, they have no energy, they are usually ill—they catch every sickness, cold and flu that comes along. When they catch it, it is difficult to rid themselves of it. They are advocates of medicine and surgery as their first choice of action because they see it as more expedient and "easier" route to "getting well". In fact, a great many of these people do not even know what being well means. It has been so long since they have experienced wellness, they have nothing to compare with their present state of being.

Many people at the bottom of the health gradient may be on the verge of death. Drugs and surgical intervention may be justified in their health care program, simply to keep them alive. If they live they might get the idea that their bodies are enough or that they can recover their innate health. Maybe they will realize that their bodies are functioning, continually replacing cells every year, producing new and healthy tissues. They just might realize that they can actually get well.

You can see why many of the people at the bottom of the health gradient are on the verge of death. Given how they feel about themselves and life, they may as well be—dead, that is.

Now you see the two extremes of the gradient stages of health. Between these are hundreds of levels of health. What state you are experiencing varies according to how much or how little you are following the Power Health Formula.

You may be someone who eats very well but never exercises, does not sleep well and kind of prays. Or you may be somebody who never eats well, drinks tons of water, gets a little bit of sleep, does a lot of exercise and does not have any visualization or prayer techniques. You can be any combination of these.

114

Starting to get the picture why there is no one silver bullet solution to optimal health? The more parts of the Formula that you are using, the higher up the health gradient you are. To the degree that you are following more of the health care laws of the Power Health Formula, you will be above the gradient median and in fairly decent health. To the degree that you are using fewer of the laws, you will be below the median and, more frequently than not, feeling crappy.

So, if your local, multi-level marketing genius comes to your door with the latest cure for everything, and if you, as I have often done, purchase their products just simply to get rid of them, those of you that are lower on the health gradient will probably experience some sort of an improvement. Why not? You have nowhere to go but up.

If you are not eating well, not drinking enough fluids, not getting enough exercise, not sleeping, and not getting any light, guess what? If you improve your system in *any way*, you will have to feel better. This is why, in my practice, about 20% to 30% of the multi-level marketing vitamin users will experience almost immediate positive results. They will regard their improvement as a miracle then go out and tout their product as being the most wonderful product that has ever been produced in the history of the world. Sometimes these products will get them so excited that they will unknowingly focus their mind and believe that they are going to get well of various types sicknesses and diseases and those beliefs *will* manifest in them getting well (remember the mind body connection). This phenomenon ultimately culminates in the miracle testimonials you hear regarding every new wonder product that hits the market. The product fulfills a deficiency in the fuel part of that person's physiology and engages the mind body healing affect. So these products are neither all bad nor all good. They, however, are *never* the silver bullet.

This is how health works. The lower down the gradient of health you are, the more likely it is that you are going to need more radical intervention and outside help. If you are at the bottom of the health gradient and your body is going to give out after fifty years of abuse, surgical or medical intervention may be appropriate. Possibly after the heroic interventions of drugs, surgery, herbs, vitamins and other

115

potions you will survive to begin fueling your body well, drinking water, sleeping, using your mind and reversing the deterioration process. Conversely, the higher up on the gradient you are, the less intervention it will take for you to improve whatever problem you are experiencing. I see this phenomenon unfold daily in my chiropractic practice. People at the top of the health gradient scale get well from their health conditions more frequently and quickly than those on the health gradient steps below.

This last observation was a major factor in convincing me to author this book. I have always wanted my patients not only to get well, but to do so quickly. Prior to creating the Power Health Formula multimedia program, I presented a weekly class in the basic principles, which led to its formulation to aid my chiropractic patients' tissues to heal more quickly. I taught these principles to as many as would listen and the results spoke for themselves. The people who attended the class indeed had far more successful—and less expensive—recoveries.

A lot of people ask me how and why a chiropractor came up with a formula that extended so far beyond the range of information relative to correcting spinal conditions. Let me put that question in the context of my professional experience with patients and healing.

When people come to my office, they are bent over, unable to move, experiencing joint problems in their spines, knees, ankles, shoulders and just about everywhere else. They are in this condition because they have not followed several components of the Power health Formula. In particular they have ignored the components of exercise and diet. Most of these people have stopped moving. Remember, motion is life. You must keep those joints moving.

As chiropractors we work with the *body's* ability to heal. So the success of our treatment depends a great deal on the health of that patient's mind, body and spirit. The Power Health Formula began as a lecture to educate people on how to get up that gradient of health and get better results from my treatments. The higher on the scale patients are, the more quickly they heal. By educating patients on the fact that what they drank, what they ate, how they slept and how they thought had a positive effect on their soft tissues and thus on our treatments, we accomplished many things. But the original focus of the class was simply to allow our chiropractic treatments to be more effective.

Again, my clinical observation is that the closer to the top of the gradient of health a patient is when they come into the office, the better their body responded to treatment. Their joints are easy to manipulate because their tissues are healthy. They have a positive mental attitude. They come in expecting to get well and they do.

Relative to the topic of response to care, it has been my experience that people whose bodies are close to the bottom of the health gradient do not respond to any type of care well due to years of dietary abuse, being sedentary, not getting any sleep and having a negative mental attitude. I almost don't want to accept their cases. I have to sit down with these folks and explain to them that their chances of getting better are okay as long as they are willing to understand that it is going to take a great deal of time, effort on their part and much cooperation. Interestingly enough, most people at this lower end of the scale do not want to put forth any effort or take responsibility for their recovery. Big surprise!

Regarding the area of bodywork, posture and integrated highways, people lower on the gradient scale generally need some outside intervention to help them get started up. I found that if you are very, very low on the health gradient in terms of your physical being (i.e. your bones, your muscles) you will need to see a chiropractor, a massage therapist, a rolfer, or any of the body workers that are out there working with these tissues. Once you regain a certain degree of flexibility and function, however, you should be able to take over the project of rehabilitating your physical body yourself through exercising.

That is how you should use outside intervention. Assess approximately where you feel you are on the health gradient, given the information that you now have about the Power Health Formula. Then decide whether outside intervention is appropriate for you in that part of the Power Health Formula you are trying to master.

117

Use the intervention until you can handle that area of the Formula on your own. That help might be vitamins and minerals, some sort of biofeedback to help you sleep or an outside spiritual source to help you pray. If you are at the bottom, the road up is so long. If it seems overwhelming, by all means begin with outside help. Do whatever it takes to get going. If you need help deciding what is appropriate, refer to the Power Health website (www.powerhealthnet.com) or contact us with your health history and we can help get you on your way. Having said that, there is a point, as you come up the gradient, that <u>you</u> must start to take your Power back.

This leads me to the practitioners who try to sell you on the idea that you need to be in their office, ostensibly for "prevention" for the rest of your life. I enjoy a massage once a month because I feel it really helps me out due to the physical demands of my job. I also will get an occasional manipulation from my chiropractor. Other than that, I pretty much run my own health program and I will tell you, I am at the top of the health gradient. I rarely become ill. On the very rare occasions when I am out of balance and I become ill, I will usually get over an illness in a day that takes most people weeks to overcome. I do it all myself.

Trust me. I was a very ill child. I was not healthy. Medicine, drugs and surgeries were a part of my life. My paradigm was very negative. I did have the advantage of always being one to exercise. But I was also one who was sold on the fact that sleep was not a great thing. I was low on the scale but I have worked my way up.

So when a doctor says you need to see him/her forever, you have two choices. Choice number one is walk. Find another doctor that will help you with the area of the Power Health Formula you are dealing with. Find one that will help you to *not* need future services. Your other choice is stick with the doctor until you have reached a point in your exercise, sleep, diet, etc. at which you feel confident to manage your own life. Then walk. You need to take back the Power. That 'you' part is the whole point of the Power Health Formula.

The Power Health Formula Program has been formulated for you, not only through using the clinical experiences of thousands of patients but from my own personal experience climbing up the gradient of health. I know where you are, what you are feeling, your fears, concerns and what you need. The Formula handles it all.

The Formula is basic. The Formula is simple. Implementation is not *always* easy but it is inexpensive and doable. That is why we supply you with an affirmation tape to emphasize the mental part of the Power Health Formula. It is all you will ever need.

As you climb the health gradient you will begin to feel the Power. The Power makes you self-sufficient. You are all you need ant that realization is an intoxicating experience. It is something that I wish each human being could experience at some point in their life. Once you experience it, there is no going back.

Now you should understand that the Power Health Formula is a law. Hopefully you agree that you are a part of an evolving universe and the laws of the universe apply to you. You are now aware of health gradients. You can approximate where you are on the gradient of health, or you can contact us to help you with this matter. Knowing that there is no magic bullet, you are ready to implement the program in its entirety.

We are all so different. Each of us is at a different stage on the gradient of health. It takes a Formula. So let's move on to helping you implement the Power Health Formula.

Implementation of the Power Health Formula

Critical point. We are all that we need. All that we are and all that we need to have, all that we want and all that we can be is provided within our physical bodies, our intellectual minds, our spiritual beings and by our environment.

I would like to take just a moment to review how the equation works so that you can get it "<u>FIRM</u>"ly in your mind that this equation is all that you need to focus on to achieve optimum wellness. Understanding the Formula's full implications is the first step to implementing the Formula.

F is for FUELS. If you put the proper fuels in your body, it will work optimally. In addition to providing nutrition, the proper foods will detoxify, cleanse, give you plenty of antioxidants and probably hundreds of other essential, nutritional elements which dieticians and scientists have not yet even discovered. Proper food (fuel) will increase your energy, improve your immune system and decrease your allergies. But the main thing eating well will do is give your body the proper high-octane fuels to operate at its optimum capacity and capability.

Drink water. It is a component of the intake of proper fuels. Water detoxifies the system. Along with proper diet, water encourages weight loss and weight balance. It is an anti-aging substance and it decreases stress. Water allows your system to operate properly and is a contributor to beautiful and clear skin.

Get outside and experience the proper sunlight. You will again experience detoxification through more of the proper fuels. You will experience energy, be able to sleep more soundly and notice improvements in many aspects of your metabolism including the calcium, vitamin D vitamin pathways. Exposure to sunlight will even reduce stress and help you eliminate depression.

Breathe correctly. Oxygen is another fuel component that holds obvious benefits as those of you have found that have occasionally tried to go without! Proper breathing techniques bring three times more oxygen into the body, giving the cells more of the basic fuels that they need. Proper breathing techniques also move your lymph fluids and detoxify your system. Breath control helps the blood to circulate better and massages your organs. Deep breathing keeps your bowels moving and, along with the other fuels, it gives your body the optimum, high-octane, perfect fuels for your perfectly, exquisitely designed body to be able to operate maximally in its environment.

I is for interconnected highways. Interconnected highways have to do with keeping your muscles, joints, ligaments, tendons and other soft tissues of your body healthy so that you can achieve improved posture. Improved posture and normally functioning joints and soft tissues keep pressure off the nervous system, allowing your nervous systems interconnected highways to deliver the maximum nerve supply to every cell in your body. Improved posture also allows your blood to flow freely, your organs to function better, and your body to breathe better. Proper posture and joint function allows you to assimilate all fuels better. It keeps your joints from getting irritated, reduces arthritis, aids indigestion, reduces pressure on your heart and allows proper, easier bowel elimination.

R is for rest. Sleep does many of the same things that the fuels and the integrated highways do. Sleep detoxifies your system by regulating your digestive system. Sleep enables your mind to work better by allowing it to recycle necessary neurochemicals. Sleep regulates your immune system. Together with proper nerve supply

121

and proper food it further strengthens your immune system. This ultimately allows your body to work appropriately in its environment and enables it to fight off the sicknesses and diseases that it has already been programmed to fight off.

Sleep is affected by the first two components of the Formula, as each part of the Formula affects every other. If you are eating the proper fuels, you will sleep better. If you are putting fuels in your body that alter your physiology (i.e. foods that contain excessive amounts of nicotine, caffeine, alcohol) you will sleep poorly. Proper foods help sleep.

Finally, **M** is for the mind. The mind may be the most important aspect of this program. We now know that the mind itself and its thoughts communicates through neuropeptides with every single cell of your body, not only controlling the functioning of your cells but more than likely actually affecting the genetic determination of you and your offspring. We all know that if a person gets depressed their immune system depresses and they tend to get every sickness and disease known to man. The mind affects every aspect of sleep. A peaceful, calm mind and a peaceful, calm being will allow for better sleep. It will allow the nerve supply to rejuvenate. It will allow better food digestion.

It would take another book to completely exemplify how each component of the Formula affects interacts with each other component of the Formula. But, hopefully, you get the idea. You cannot get Power Health by following only one part of the Formula. Eventually you must incorporate the entire equation into your life.

Put all the components of the Power Health Formula together and the cumulative effects are exponential. What you achieve is a maximally operating body with optimal physiological cellular function. Remember, your health is a direct reflection of your cellular physiology.

This is the goal. This is what we are trying to achieve. Maximum cellular function and a maximally healthy body will allow you to enjoy your life and see every day as a positive.

But how do you go about implementing the Power Health Formula?

The first step is to **understand** how your body works. If, at this point, you do not have an understanding of how your body works, how it breaks down, how it gets well, and the fact that you are in control when utilizing all elements of the Power Health Formula depending on where you are on your gradient of health, then I would suggest that you first review this entire book before you go on to the next step.

The next step is to **prioritize**. At this point in the evolution of mankind, our lives are quite complex. We, as a society, believe that more is better. We think that we are missing out if we are not experiencing every aspect of everything that is presented to us in the media or by our friends and family. *News flash!!* The media and your friends are not looking out for you. They are looking out for themselves. Do not buy their manipulation.

You must simplify and prioritize. By prioritizing I mean you need to decide what is most important to you. I have very few aspects of my life that I address every day. The elements of life that are most important to me are:

Me. I cannot help anyone if I am not feeling well, if I am sick, if I am not energetic and if I am not focused. I cannot accomplish much without focus and I lose confidence. If I am not confident, my family and my patients are the ones that suffer.

My health, mental, physical and spiritual health, is my number one priority.

My family.

My business.

My recreation. All of that goes to help me with my number five priority.

My contribution to mankind.

I find that by simply focusing on these simple, basic priorities, I experience a fullness of life, a joy, an efficiency and an effectiveness that very few people ever obtain. You must prioritize what is important in your life. Then focus on those elements and forget the rest.

I assume health is high on your list or you would not have invested in this program. Sit down with a pencil and a paper. Write down everything in your life that you feel is important to you now. Number them from one to whatever in the order of priority. Pick out the top five or six and go for it.

Again, if you are going to implement the Power Health Formula, you better make sure that having a healthy mind and body are in the top six priorities or you will not integrate the Formula into your life.

The next step is to **decide**. You need to decide to take action. This is a very personal matter and it is for this reason that we have developed the Power Health Formula Workbook as well as the affirmation tapes. Deciding to be healthy is a sticking point for a great many people. Making change is not easy. You must decide to make a change. You are about to go into unfamiliar territory. That can be scary. It can put you in fear and it can put you in doubt.

The second CD in the Power Health Formula program is specifically designed for you to use when you are driving, when you are exercising, when you have down time or when you are feeling any kind of doubt whatsoever. If you are feeling doubtful, just pop this CD in and listen. It will inspire you, it will focus you and it will enable you to deal with those aspects of your belief systems and your value systems that need to be changed in order for you to move on with this program.

The last step of implementing the Power Health Formula is, of course, to **take action**. There is no thought in this universe, there is no affirmation or visualization or prayer that will manifest in the physical universe until you take action. There are several types of affirmations. There are affirmations of word, there are affirmations of thought, there are affirmations of feeling and there are affirmations of essence. We have presented you with affirmations of thought and of word. But the most powerful affirmation in the world is the affirmation of essence. That means the affirmation of action. You must become who and what you say you are. To do that, your actions must follow your words and your thoughts. The affirmations that we have provided will start you down the road of action and they will help you to overcome fears and doubts and other obstacles along the way. But you must begin to take action.

How do you do that? My suggestion is to look at the Power Health Formula. Find some aspect of the Formula that you have already implemented into your life. If you are a good sleeper, go to the sleep section first. If you find that drinking water appeals to you, start drinking more water first. Implementing positive change begins when you take action on what is for you, a small and simple challenge. Then you overcome and master that challenge. As you overcome each challenge you will gain more and more Power and more and more incentive to go on to the next level of challenge. Each level of challenge will become easier and easier. Actually, it will become fun.

But you must take action. Begin with what's simple for you. Improve. Enjoy success. Move on to a more challenging part of the Formula. If you have trouble, the Power Health Formula™ workbook walks you through the process step by step with goal sheets, priority sheets, daily and weekly work sheets. Order forms are located at the back of the book.

Know that this is a process. This is a journey. This is an unfolding of a path. Enjoy the journey, even the bumps. Every night before you go to bed, focus on the *victories* that you had that day, no matter how small they may be. Whether it was drinking five glasses of water instead of three, or getting seven hours of sleep instead of five. Continue to focus on your victories and continue to focus on the journey. This will lead you up the gradient of the Power Health Scale and to the Promised Land of absolute optimum health.

Order Form

QTY	Title	Price	Total
	Dr. Martin Rutherford's Power Health Formula video/cd package	$99.95	
	Shipping and Handling $5 for all orders in the US		
	Sales tax (NV state residents only, add 7.25%)		
	Total Enclosed		

Telephone Orders:
Call 1-877-901-9037
Have your VISA or
MasterCard ready.

Postal Orders:
Power Health Network, Inc
1175 Harvard Way
Reno, NV 89502

Web Orders:
Go to www.powerhealthnet.com

Method of Payment:
❑ Check
❑ VISA
❑ MasterCard

Card #:_____
Expiration Date:_____
Signature:_____

Name: _____
Address: _____
City: _____ State: _____ Zip: _____
Daytime Phone: _____

Quantity discounts are available.
Call 1-877-901-9037 for more information

About the Author

Dr. Rutherford, an ex two sport collegiate athlete who injured himself to the point of disability, was told by numerous doctors he would be in a wheel chair by the age of 30. His journey back to health caused him to choose health care as his field and culminated in his earning his doctorate of chiropractic in 1979. Dr Rutherford is currently the clinic director of Power Health Integrated Wellness Center; a practice of diverse alternative and medical health professionals. Dr. Rutherford's clinical observations have led to the irrevocable conclusion that the healing power is within each of us. Now the picture of health Dr Rutherford has also produced several CDs, cassettes, and videos on health, has been interviewed on numerous TV and radio shows, and continues to lecture to the public on a wide variety of health issues.

51382363R00093

Made in the USA
San Bernardino, CA
20 July 2017